RUNNING PAST MIDNIGHT

Enjoying the Himalayas

RUNNING PAST MIDNIGHT

A Woman's Ultra-Marathon Adventure

Molly Sheridan

with **Al Marquis**

For information contact:
Molly Sheridan
molly@desertskyadventures.com

ISBN hardcover: 978-1-939758-65-1
ISBN paperback: 978-1-939758-66-8
ISBN ebook: 978-1-939758-67-5

Cover Photo: Justin Yurkanin
Cover Design: Devin Sheridan and Dreamz, Inc.

CONTENTS

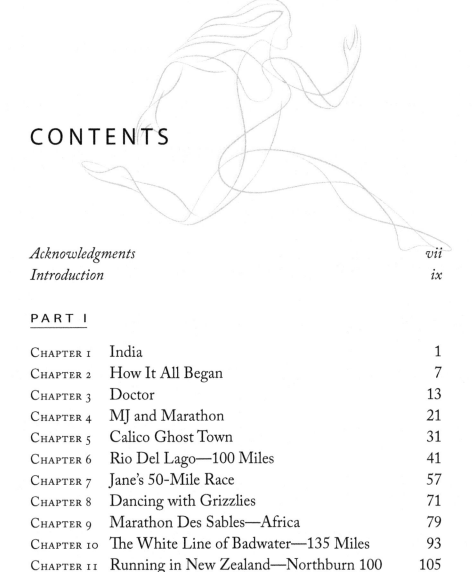

ACKNOWLEDGMENTS

THANK YOU TO my wonderful, talented sister Colleen, whose daily words of encouragement filled me with inspiration. I would never have finished this book without her wise counsel and unending support. She is my best friend and my twin, even though she was born fifteen months before me. My life is so much more enriched and beautiful because of her.

Kylie Johnson, you made a phone call to me that completely changed my life for the better. Thank you for teaching me that running is fun!

Devin Sheridan, you are not only the best son a mom could ever have, you are also an amazingly talented artist. Thank you for creating the book cover and for all the projects I incessantly hand over to you! You are a major support to my life in more ways than I can express.

Bailey Sheridan, my adorable, oldest daughter. I credit both my successful finishes at Badwater and La Ultra—The High to you as my crew chief. You are the most excellent, hard-working, and FUN crewmember ever. Thank you for getting me to the finish line under overwhelmingly tough circumstances.

Taylor Sheridan, my amazing daughter, who, when I first wrote this book, was a hilarious, wild teen whose drama knew no bounds. I am happy to report that you are now a mature woman who is STILL hilarious and adorably wild. Thank you for adding all the fun and excitement to so many of my adventures.

Kim Dean, how can I ever thank you for the weeks and months of your careful and meticulous typing of this book? Plus, your wonderful feedback that I so needed! I am thankful for your patience and generous spirit.

Thank you, friend, confidant, lawyer, and author, Al Marquis, for taking an interest in my life, for understanding my quirkiness, and for having faith and confidence in me.

Finally, thank you, Bill Andrews, my adorable "Buddy." Life with you is always a grand adventure.

Molly Sheridan

INTRODUCTION

I HAVE BEEN friends with Molly Sheridan for twenty-five years, but somewhere in the middle we lost contact with each other. When we happened to join mutual friends for lunch, I asked her what she had been doing.

"Running," she said with a smile.

Well, maybe we have something in common, I thought to myself. After all, I have been a runner my whole life. I've run a couple of 10Ks. Once I even ran 10 miles. "So how far have you been running?" I asked.

"One hundred-mile ultramarathons," Molly casually responded.

I nearly fell out of my chair. Molly is slender and six feet tall, and I never knew her to engage in athletic activities. I stuttered and stammered . . . I wanted to know more.

Like most of you, I had no idea what was involved in running 100 miles. Participants run through the night, sometimes in wilderness areas. They risk mountain lions, bears, and rebel soldiers in foreign countries. They have to eat, drink, and change clothes while running. A whole crew is necessary to support them. At the stroke of midnight, when the rest of us are sleeping in our warm, peaceful beds, runners like Molly, who are out to test their personal limits, keep right on running.

Al Marquis

Part I

CHAPTER 1

India

"Adventure, yeah. I guess that's what you call it when
everyone comes back alive."

—Mercedes Lackey, *Spirits White as Lightning*

I RAN DOWN the road toward the sunrise. The long, thin red glow of light at the horizon lifted my spirits. The familiar euphoria, the joy of running, swelled inside me. It was cold and brisk, but my running tights and jacket insulated me from the bite of the snowy mountain air. I was elated to emerge from eight hours of darkness. The energy from the sun radiated down to my feet and propelled me forward.

The city of Leh appeared in the distance. A large Buddhist monastery was perched above the city, one of sixteen monasteries in the region. The temple was carved centuries ago into the side of a mountain. Golden Buddha statues adorned with flowers and silk scarves embellished the structure. Prayer flags decorated the rooftop, and the wind blew hundreds of colorful pieces of fabric, like so many shimmering rainbows, over the towers. I was awed by the majestic beauty.

My legs and body felt strong as I flew down the hillside. It was a rush compared to yesterday, when I trudged up the enormous mountain pass and into the night.

Suddenly a little van pulled up alongside me. A young blond driver stuck his head out the window and said, "Hey, are you Molly?"

"Yes, I am Molly." I laughed out loud. I was in the middle of nowhere, in India near the border of China and Pakistan, running a 138-mile race in the Himalayas. Human beings were few and far between, especially blond guys who spoke English. I did a double-take to check out the vehicle and make sure I wasn't hallucinating. Did this guy really just ask if I was Molly?

"My name is Ben," he yelled out the window as the van rolled beside me. "I am a reporter from the Christian Science Monitor. Can I interview you?"

I must have had the most dumbfounded look on my face. "Are you kidding? How did you find me?" Ben told me he was covering the political conflict in Kashmir, a hundred miles away. His editor heard about the race and asked him to cover the event. I panted, "You can interview me, if you can run."

Ben whipped his van to the side of the road, jumped out with voice recorder and camera in hand, and ran to catch up with me. He was half my age (if that). Ben said he had been driving all over trying to find me. Finally, Dr. Rajat Chauhan, the race director, directed him to my location.

"The race started yesterday and you have been on the course for twenty hours," he panted, "How are you doing?"

"I'm awesome," I replied. "How are you?"

"I heard you had some challenges with an avalanche yesterday," he asked, adjusting his camera strap over his shoulder as he ran.

"Yes, there was an avalanche on the first peak. But I was more worried about the live hand grenade I found next to me in the snow when I sat on a rock for a quick rest." I slowed my pace a bit because his cheeks were turning bright red.

"No kidding!" He ran past me, snapped a photo and ran back. "What did you do with the grenade? And what is it like to run at 18,000 feet?"

"I left the grenade alone, and running at 18,000 feet is frickin' hard!" I smiled. I was giddy from the flowing endorphins. I was thrilled that I'd conquered the first 18,000-foot peak, and I was even happier to be in sunshine. The night had been dramatic and scary. Ben was charming and reminded me of my own son Devin, who was close to the same age. I wondered what had caused Ben to come to such a wild place to write about wars and runners.

"I read that you are a self-proclaimed scaredy-cat," he continued. "How is that possible? Here you are in a race that has never been attempted."

"Where did you hear that?" I retorted. Colleen, I think, was the only person I had confided in to that extent. "I try not to think about fear," I laughed, "unless, of course, I have a reporter asking me about it as we run through the Himalayas."

"Is it true that you didn't start running until a couple of years ago? Age forty-eight? I am sure you have people questioning your sanity," he proclaimed with a grin.

"Yes, some people say I am crazy; too old to be running; not athletic enough; too tall ... I've heard it all. I suppose I could stay home and watch the Kardashians." I laughed again, feeling happy.

"Do you have children?" He sounded a little winded. "If so, what do they think of their mother running in a remote area of the Himalayas?"

"I have three adorable kids. My son Devin is twenty-nine, my daughters Bailey and Taylor are teenagers. They are my greatest adventure. They are super-excited about my running."

Well, I thought to myself, sometimes they are excited. I had dragged Taylor to my first 100-mile race event kicking and screaming. Taylor groaned, "Oh, my gawd, Mom," rolling her eyes with plenty of drama and attitude. "Running is sooooooo boring! Do I have to sit and wait for you alllllll night?!"

I had asked her to help crew my first 100-mile non-stop race in Northern California. The crew rendezvouses with the runner at various designated stations and helps with food and supplies. I thought it would be a good experience for her and instill the love of the great outdoors.

"Where will the bathrooms be when I meet you on the trail?" she demanded with her hand propped on her hip.

"My dear daughter, there are not any bathrooms. We are in the middle of the forest," I replied calmly.

"What! Are you joking?" She was incredulous. Bailey rolled her eyes behind her. "Not cool, Mom!" she gasped, "Where do you expect me to go?"

"Taylor, nature is all around you." I said with a smile, "Carry a packet of tissues!"

Taylor shot me a look of exasperation. At the 20-mile aid station, Bailey pulled me aside. "Mom, you aren't going to leave me with her the whole time, are you? She is already starting to bug me!"

"Bailey, I am sure the two of you will work it out. Your mother needs to go and run another 80 miles."

I smiled to myself as my thoughts returned to Ben the reporter. He continued his interview. "Do your kids ever worry about you?" he asked.

Hmmmm, I had to think about that one. I had told them that I was entering the race, but I hadn't mentioned the fact that 138 miles in the Himalayas had never before been attempted. I also omitted the stern opinion of several physicians that we were risking death by running over 18,000-foot peaks. Nor did I mention terrorists in nearby Afghanistan. They reacted to my announcement like I was returning to run Badwater in Death Valley, only three hours from our Las Vegas home. What would my kids do if they heard I was lost in the Himalayas? Bailey would probably want to punch someone in the face. Taylor would get completely hysterical; her drama would be so profound that everyone would forget that I was missing. (I always thought that acting classes would be good for her.) Devin, 6-feet-7-inches of quiet strength, would calm his sisters and methodically organize the search party. I cast such thoughts from my mind.

"What are some of the other challenges that you have faced in this race?" Ben continued.

At those sobering words, I stared straight ahead, gathering my thoughts as my shoes tapped on the road. Do I tell him about last night's drama? The struggle up the mountain? Heaving my guts out on the side of the road? I turned and eyeballed Ben holding his voice recorder. We were running in sync. "I am trying not to think about challenges right now," I smiled, keeping my pace relaxed as I evaded his question. "I am moving one step at a time."

After running two miles, Ben, with sweat rolling down his face, told me he was finished running. He promised to come find me on the course the next day to check my progress and ask more questions. "When I see you tomorrow," he gasped, "I want to know why you started running. Think about that and I'll catch up!"

I watched him walk back toward his little van as I jogged down the quiet road. I never saw Ben again. I learned later that he ended up back in Kashmir, after getting lost on the race course after a snowstorm hit. He did email me months later to wrap up our discussion.

My conversation with the reporter left me with thoughts about my kids. I missed all three of them. I tucked them safely away in my heart. I had a long way to go.

The next town was Choglamsar, the summer home of the Dalai Lama. I had seen the Dalai Lama walking around the streets of Leh in the weeks that I spent acclimating before the race. I hoped

I would see him again. The monks fascinated me. The townspeople were so lovable. I was falling in love with India. I took a deep breath and settled back into my running rhythm.

I thought about Ben's question: Why did I start running? It seemed so long ago and so far away. It was a different life, or was it? I settled into my run and let my thoughts float back. I remembered a phone call a few years back. . . .

CHAPTER 2

How It All Began

"If you think you are too small to make a difference,
try sleeping with a mosquito."
—His Holiness The Dalai Lama

MY HOME PHONE was ringing on a Thursday night. I almost didn't pick it up because I was tired from working all day. I was beat, and I really didn't feel like talking to anyone.

Kylie Johnson was on the line calling from Virginia, all the way across the U.S. She was happy and lively and took the first few minutes bringing me up to date since she moved from Las Vegas to Virginia. I worked in the Development Department with Kylie at Nevada Ballet Theatre. Kylie, who has a PhD in English, had been director of development for the ballet. Then she received an offer to join Virginia Tech. Our friendship continued long distance.

As I was casually listening to her bubbling commentary, I heard her ask, "So, do you want to train and run a marathon with me in October?"

"What?"

"Yeah. Let's do it! The Marine Corps Marathon in Washington, D.C., October."

I didn't have to think about my response. "No," I said, "No way."

I thought Kylie had lost it. Her proposal sounded so awful to me! Isn't a marathon like 25 miles or something? Don't people get really sweaty and gross? God, it sounded boring. I equated such a race to all those lemmings that run along without brains and follow each other off the cliff.

After my third or fourth "NO," Kylie pleaded, "Oh, come on. We will have FUN!"

To this day, I remember the irony of hearing the word FUN in a conversation filled with grenades. How do you fit FUN into a marathon conversation? With a final NO, I hung up. Then I laughed and thought, poor Kylie. The girl has a PhD, for God's sake! What's the matter with her?

I trudged to the kitchen, poured my customary glass of wine, and sat on the couch to watch routine TV shows. All the time I was thinking about poor, delusional Kylie.

Lying in bed that night, I thought about Kylie's bizarre proposal. How far is a marathon anyway? Where's the fun part? When I asked Kylie that question, she said that we would hang out together and run and walk the whole race. "We don't care how long it takes us," she proclaimed. "We just do it, and laugh our asses off."

Well, I thought, easy for her to say. She was thirty-five years old. I was about to turn fifty. She had run two marathons. I couldn't imagine running to the end of the block. I continued to toss and turn the whole night. I realized I had not worked out or exercised in forever! Then the wheels really started turning. When exactly was the last time I even took a walk? I pushed at my pillow again and rolled over. When was the last time I picked up a weight or did anything athletic? It had been a long, long time.

I started to think about how sluggish I was always feeling. Not Kylie. She was always brimming with energy. I thought about how much wine I was drinking per week, which made me feel even more inactive. I had to admit to myself that I wasn't in very good physical or mental shape.

I thought about the word FUN. I could use some FUN, no doubt about that. I also could use a big goal. I got up and Googled "marathon." Hmmm. Twenty-six-point-two miles. How hard could that be? I thought about FUN and 26.2. They didn't seem to equate, but I could pretend that it was a party. I can party.

The seed was planted, and it slowly took root and shape. My mind made the leap. Would it be possible for me? Could I do something bigger than myself?

I called Kylie the next day. "Tell me again about the FUN part," I urged. Kylie related The PLAN, and I took a leap of faith, clinging to the hope that I wasn't as wimpy as I'd always thought I was. I was nervous. I was scared. I tried to prepare myself for misery and embarrassment, but I kept coming back to the slender thread of FUN.

Training was haphazard at best. First, I did not know anyone who ran. My only link to running was Kylie, who was jumping up and down on the East Coast, telling me how fun it was going to be. I was an event planner working full time with a husband and teenage kids. I was involved in numerous community events and volunteer work. It seemed like any extra time I did have was maxed out in caring for my family, making sure everyone was fed, the dog was groomed, the house cleaned, and a million other things. As a woman, I felt it was my duty and obligation to nurture and care for my family and to give my all anytime without ever a thought about myself. My days were completely filled. So I couldn't figure out how in the world I was going to carve out time for workouts. What were the workouts, and how the heck could I go from weak and un-athletic to running even a mile? The thought of running more than a mile wasn't even registering in my brain. I was trying to figure out what it was like to get to the start line. How do I begin?

Kylie told me to go online and look up Jeff Galloway. Jeff is an Olympic athlete and marathon runner, who wrote a great book on how to run your first marathon. His philosophy was to walk and run and ease into the training. As I started to immerse myself in online training, I noticed that I was back at the computer continuously to learn everything I could about running. As I dove further into the mysterious world of running, I began to feel an inner spark, a resolve that began to take shape and stir inside me. I was getting excited about this new adventure. My life was taking on a new purpose. It was scary but also thrilling. I thought, what if? What if I could really do this thing? My connection to Kylie gave me the confidence I needed to move toward the goal. I tried not to think about the fact that Kylie was half my age. That thought had to be continually suppressed when it crept into my consciousness.

My first attempt at running was horrible. I put on my running shoes, shorts, and a T-shirt and tried to look the part. I bought a runner's logbook and turned to page one. I wrote down two miles before I even ran, because I was not going to come back to the house unless it was completed. (I had marked off two miles in my car on the way home from buying my logbook.) I wanted to fill all the pages with miles and miles and get moving! Stepping out the door, I looked around the empty street. I was happy that none of my neighbors was outside to witness my debut in my brand new running outfit, faking my way around the neighborhood streets trying to look like a real runner. I thought if I just got out there and ran ran ran, I would somehow magically transform into a runner. Checking out my digital watch, I wanted to see how long I could run. I took off down the street towards the park...10 seconds. Not bad, heart pumping...20 seconds...I can do this, okay...30 seconds...holy crap...45 seconds...argh, gagging, panting...50 seconds...geezuz! I could not imagine running two minutes. I wanted to force myself to get to the point I had read about, the runner's "high." There had to be some payoff somewhere, and I wanted to get there fast because so far this was not FUN! Since I did not know what I was doing, I started running, panting, dying, going up the sidewalk, feeling miserable, trying to break through the nauseous fatigue. Where was the effortless love of running? It had to be out there somewhere.

After fifteen minutes, I stopped, turned around, and walked back to the house, depressed and dejected. I looked at the schedule I had printed out to train for the marathon. The paper itself was daunting with the miles laid out for the entire week. Somehow I would have to trick my mind into making this more fun. So I began to focus on moving through space. I needed to put my mind to work to make this enjoyable and filled with purpose.

The next day, and every morning thereafter, I got up, threw on my running shoes and made my way out into the street. The first twenty minutes was always the worst. I always felt sluggish and exhausted after a minute or two. I mostly walked and tried to keep my heart rate under control so it wasn't pounding through my chest. I needed this race. I wanted to conquer my goal. After a few days, the realization of how much I needed this dawned on me. I was approaching fifty years old. My kids were leaving for college. My life as a mom at home raising children was over. What was I going to do with the second half of my life? The first half had been pretty good. I loved raising my kids. I realized that my marriage might not make the transition. I loved my husband and we had successfully created an awesome family. But life is full of changes, and I didn't know what the future would hold for us. I wanted answers and the running turned on a switch inside that seemed to open my mind and calm it. Answers came to me out on that pavement as I was trudging through my neighborhood. I marveled at houses and trees that I'd never noticed before. I found calmness and peace. My mind opened up on those morning runs. The movement lifted my spirit and filled me with power. I took deep breaths and filled my lungs. I began to love the dark mornings right before sunrise. Every morning was a secret adventure on the quiet streets, listening to the rhythmic tapping of my shoes on the pavement. I actually found myself looking forward to those morning excursions. I wanted to run and run and run. I wanted to keep running in order to hold on to the feeling of freedom and movement. I'd generally get back to the house before anyone was awake. I'd pull out that sacred piece of paper listing all my miles, and I would check off the day, the time, and those amazing miles I had captured.

My schedule became my focus. On mornings that I didn't feel the pull to leave my warm bed, I tricked my mind and refused to negotiate with the comfortable warm spot. I instead envisioned my inner Goddess, the Warrior Goddess that I created while out there running alone. She was no-nonsense and stronger than me. She could kick ass if I hesitated any longer, and I trusted her judgment.

Soon I was out the door and running alone in the dark. I thought about my husband and kids comfortably tucked in their beds but not with envy. I thought of them with satisfaction and Warrior Goddess self-esteem. My family was safe and sound while I was out battling the elements on my own in the twilight of the morning. I turned a corner and ran down a street I had never entered before. I saw the blue hue of the morning news through my neighbors' French windows as I glided by. I forgave myself out there. One day at a time, my inner spirit told me, just keep moving and the answers will come.

CHAPTER 3

Doctor

"Remember that sometimes not getting what you
want is a wonderful stroke of luck."
—His Holiness The Dalai Lama

I WAS A complete rookie in every way, and so it is not surprising that five weeks into training, I got a stress fracture. This injury was not due to Jeff Galloway and the online training. If I would have listened to his books and read them properly, my injury would have been avoided.

One day I began to feel a pain in my left foot. I refused to listen to the incessant yelling from my ankle for me to stop and take a break. The new discovery of running had brought me a taste of pure freedom, and as with any drug, I was overloading with wild abandon and pushing my body where it wasn't ready to go.

First, I ignored the screaming ankle and thought it would go away. Two days later, however, I realized my ankle was swollen and that I needed to go and have it checked out. So I hopped in the car and went to a doctor whom I'd found in the yellow pages, an orthopedic guy. I remember sitting in his waiting room thinking, this cannot be that bad, I mean, you know, I probably did a stupid thing piling on all those miles in a week. I just need to soak it or something and get back to training as soon as possible. My whole mindset, as

I sat there in the doctor's office, was the intense realization that I really wanted to run in the upcoming marathon. My attitude had somehow turned 180 degrees from dread into a burning desire. I had a new goal, and it had become vitally important. When they ushered me into the doctor's office, I was embarrassed, certain that I had taken the trip to the office prematurely. It couldn't be that bad.

After the x-ray, I sat waiting for the doctor in his cold, white exam room. A young guy with a lab coat walked in and snapped the x-ray onto the lighted screen. I thought he was an orderly, he looked so young.

Without looking at me he said, "You have a stress fracture."

I was stunned. "I do? Really, you are sure?"

"Yes," he replied, "you definitely have a stress fracture. What are you doing?"

He turned towards me, seemingly preoccupied and bored. It was then that I realized that he was my doctor.

I responded with my newly adopted Warrior Goddess positive attitude. "Oh wow, you know what? I am training for a marathon, and I cannot believe I got a stress fracture. I just started training!" I smiled nervously and tried to connect with him.

The doc cocked his head, scowled at me, and asked, "How old are you?"

"I am forty-eight."

He took down the x-ray, closed it in a folder, and said, "You are too old to be running a marathon. Pick a different sport."

I was so shocked at those words I did not know what to say. The Warrior Goddess began to falter.

"Oh, no," I burst out. "No. This is important. You can't tell me that. I am excited about this race. I need to run it!"

"No." He shook his head dismissively. "This is not for you. Look at what you've done to yourself. Forty-eight is too old."

I felt my face heating up, and I had the overwhelming urge to kick him in the ankle. I wanted to make his ankle feel like mine. I wanted to scream at him but concluded that he would simply view me as a raving old woman.

Instead, I took a deep breath and attempted to internally calm myself from the shock of it all. I had never felt old my entire life until that very moment. Is forty-eight old? My head was reeling. I sat up a little taller and fought the overwhelming urge to punch him in the face. The mental images of me turning into Muhammad Ali and getting little baby face Dr. Mean into the ring made me feel better. Another deep breath. . . .

"Well," I calmly stated, "you know what? Honestly, I have been reading all about running, and I know that if you do have a stress fracture, you can get into a pool and do pool running. I can continue to train through this stress fracture." I Google-searched that myself, you complete idiot!

"No. Put a boot on," he sighed. "We are not going to talk about that. You are out of action for six weeks."

I took another deep breath. "Well, what do I do for six weeks while my stress fracture is recouping? I want to stay in shape."

He dismissed me with a wave of his hand and said, "Come back and talk to me in six weeks." With that, he abruptly turned and left the room.

I sat there, numb and upset. I could not comprehend that this guy was not going to listen to me. I had used all my reserve to stay calm and be reasonable. Now I wanted to kill him. Or cry.

The nurse came in holding the boot that I would need to wear every day for six weeks. As she began to strap on the boot, I felt like someone was attaching a ball and chain to my life. As I stiffened, she looked up at me kindly. Big tears were welling up in my eyes, and I was having trouble maintaining my composure.

"Oh, honey." The nurse patted my arm. "You are going to be fine."

I looked at her for moral support. "I cannot believe that the doctor says I should not do anything for six weeks!" My shoulders started shaking with anger and frustration. If I did nothing for six weeks, I would be back where I started. All that training for nothing. It would be impossible for me to finish a marathon which was scheduled for October, five months away. I needed every day of the five months to get myself in shape.

She looked over her shoulder at the closed door. "You should go to physical therapy. There are things they can do." She gave me a big hug, and I thanked her.

I walked out of that office, dragging my foot like the mummy. Step drag, step drag, step drag. I felt like a freak, an old person dragging myself to the car. My mind was spinning. I was old? Why was I inspired with this life-changing idea to better myself, only to be stopped dead in my tracks, put in "my place" by this doctor. How could he tell me that I couldn't do something? How dare he? I climbed awkwardly into my car pulling the boot into the driver seat. (I was at least grateful that it was my left leg so I could still drive with my right foot.) The anger started to spill out of me. As I drove by the doctor's office, I screamed out the window, "DUMBSHIT!" A passing motorist gave me a concerned look. I recalled that Dr. Joyce Brothers once said that at times it is actually quite healthy to curse because it lets out stress. I screamed words I never normally use, alone in my car, grateful for any release of the awful tension. How could I have been so stupid to screw myself up? How dare that young, baby face doctor tell me that I am too old!

I was angry with him, but I was furious with myself. How could I have let this happen to my body? It seemed so stupid. I knew deep down that I hadn't been listening to my body, and it was all my fault.

I thought about age on the way home and begrudgingly admitted to myself that age had something to do with it. I was approaching fifty years. My Grandma Mac had made it to 103 and was active right up until the end. I remember her one hundredth birthday party. Half my life was over.

I had asked her, "Grandma, what does it feel like to be one hundred years old?"

"Oh, honey," she said, "don't tell anyone I'm one hundred. It's so embarrassing! Tell them I'm eighty!"

She was wearing a bright red dress and had all her makeup on and her face powdered. She opened her presents and received a bottle of perfume from her grandson, my dad. She proceeded to chase people around, laughing and spraying them. This wasn't due to dementia. On the contrary, her wits were always with her. She simply had an incredible sense of fun.

When I arrived home, both of my teenage daughters, Bailey and Taylor, were home from school and busy in the kitchen. I heard them chatting and laughing as I came around the corner wearing the boot. They both turned, looked at the boot, and burst into hysterical laughter.

Bailey could hardly speak. "Oh Mom. What in the world did you do? You look hilarious."

I started laughing as well, partly because I was so stressed out and couldn't help myself, and partly because I had pent-up nervous tension. I laughed and then I burst into tears. When I started sobbing, the laughter stopped, and they both rushed to my side. I was racked with sobs; my shoulders were shaking and my hands covered my face.

"Oh, Mom." Taylor's voice was full of concern. "We weren't making fun of you. We were laughing because your boot looks funny. Are you okay?"

"I'm okay," I sobbed, "The doctor was a total jerk and said I'm too old to be running. I am so dumb for getting a stress fracture,"

I rambled on and on about the horrible office visit while the girls exchanged looks.

Taylor was incredulous. "What? He said you are old? That's lame!"

Bailey made a face. "What crap!"

"Bailey, your language!" I exclaimed (wondering if she had read Dr. Joyce Brothers).

"Yeah, a complete idiot!" Total lame-o." They kept taking turns . . . "Dummy, stupid, nerd" . . . each name getting more and more descriptive. A teenage roast of Dr. Mean. That made me feel better.

My girls knew the effort I had made over the last few weeks getting up every morning and running through the neighborhood. At times they had joined me, but that wouldn't last long as they were finishing high school and preparing to enter college. Their older brother Devin had already graduated from college and was on his own. I knew before long I would not have any more kids at home. I would miss that more than I cared to admit. My marriage would not survive the transition. Bob had been the best husband and father. The ending of our partnership had nothing to do with him. People often commented on how we seemed to have the perfect life and family. It was a shock to everyone when we parted. To me, I simply needed time to step away from the confines of marriage and walk alone for a while. I actually wanted to think out of the box and come and go freely. I didn't want a relationship with any man. I simply wanted time for myself. I told him I wanted a year. He couldn't comprehend, and looking back, that probably wasn't fair. But I could not stop myself. I felt like I had done a pretty good job with my family. I had tried my best to fulfill their needs, to nurture them, and to enhance their lives. But after spending eighteen years in the role of wife and mother, I longed for a life of adventure and discovery. I felt a calling, but that made me wonder if I was being selfish. Yet I couldn't help myself. I had written goals in my running log. I started to think about the future and realized that the marathon goal had opened up unending possibilities in my head. I had written a bucket list. Climbing Mt. Kilimanjaro, seeing the Sahara Desert, and discovering parts of the world that I had never seen. Bob did not share my vision. He was content with his life. I certainly couldn't fault him for that.

I went to counseling to save my marriage and check my sanity. I told the therapist that I needed time for myself. Alone in the counselor's office, my therapist looked at me and laid her pencil on her notepad. "Molly," she quietly said as she gazed at me with warmth and compassion, "if you were married to any other man, we could sit here and talk about a creative relationship. You are married to a very conservative man. Your ideas of a creative relationship that is open to long periods of time alone are not going to work here. You are very brave for thinking about going it alone."

Brave? I didn't understand.

"Most women will not leave the comfort of their home even if they are unhappy. You risk losing everything." She calmly folded her hands upon her lap and let the words sink in.

"I risk losing myself if I stay," I told her.

I wanted the answers to be easier. I didn't want me or my family to go through the pain and heartache. I loved my husband. Some people told me that it was wrong to leave a person whom I loved. But I couldn't stay. Life had made a complete shift, and I found myself on the edge of a precipice. It felt like the plunge was inevitable. Either plunge or cling to the safety of the cliffs. Right or wrong, the only choice for me was to leap, out into the wind, out into the unknown depths of my heart. We stayed together for a while, but he did not join me on any of my races. It was a line that divided us that neither one of us could cross. I couldn't stop moving toward that adventure of running and somehow he couldn't join me.

<small></small>CHAPTER 4

MJ and Marathon

"Do or Do Not, there is no Try."
—Yoda

IN MY HEART and in my mind and in the depth of my soul, I wasn't fricking old. I was angry and horrified to think of that doctor telling others that they were too old, maybe crushing the spirit of those who did not have my stubbornness.

My mom always taught me to question authority. I was wishing I had her with me in the doctor's office to straighten out that doc. He would have been toast after dealing with Mary Jane Hannegan. She was a no-nonsense, Irish-Catholic mother, who raised twelve kids to be independent and self-sufficient. Six boys and six girls. We were the Irish Hannegan Clan, living in Southern California in the era of free love and Led Zeppelin. Mary Jane was always on high alert for corrupting influences. My dad, Ted, was the warm and comforting part of my childhood. I knew I could always go to him for a quick hug and smile. He was always light-hearted and easygoing. Sometimes I wished for a gentler mom. But I got Mary Jane (MJ) and she was tough.

In a family with so many people, it was easy to disappear. I never got in trouble, mostly because I learned early on to be quiet and fly under the radar. I wanted my own space, privacy, which was as rare as extra money.

21

It seemed like someone was always in trouble. I remember when my mom opened the door to two police officers when I was about fourteen years old. Mom asked, "Well, who is it now?"

The officer stepped aside to reveal my brother Matt. Matt's head was hanging low, and he was clinging to a life-size dummy that was wearing his clothes. Matt shuffled into the house ahead of the officers. The policeman explained, "Your son was on the street corner beating up this life-size dummy of himself, which was causing traffic problems."

Mom looked up at the officer and said, "Thank you, officer, we will take care of this." After the policeman left, my mom turned to Matt and said, "Well, for heaven's sake, you would think they would be out there catching criminals! Matthew, go clean up and take your good clothes off that dummy!"

Matt was guilty of a boyhood prank. This was not a major offense, so MJ moved on. But if we ever swore or stepped out of line and committed what she considered a major offense, we would suffer the wrath of Mom. We all had our chores and responsibilities. No slackers allowed.

The one time I remembered MJ's wrath was when my brother Dan made the baby, Brendan, dance naked on a table on the second floor bedroom of our home. The table was at the same level as the window. Behind our house was a school where they were having late night classes. Dan shone a light on Brendan and yelled, "DANCE!" Our adorable, two-year–old, red-headed baby brother laughed and danced up and down the table shaking all his baby fat. People from the class glanced up to the window to see a white-bellied, naked baby in a light show. Everyone in the class was pointing up at the window as Dan ducked below the window ledge, inside the bedroom, howling with laughter. All the rest of us were watching the show that Dan had orchestrated, crowded in the corner of the room, trying to muffle our laughter. That's when Mom threw open the bedroom door and snapped on the light. The baby stopped dancing. Dan stopped laughing and the rest of us gasped in horror.

"Daniel James!" she yelled as she scooped up the baby. (You knew it was bad when the second name came out and you received the Mary Jane stare.) Dan was toast. No mercy. No car. More chores. No discussion. In Mary Jane's house you obeyed the rules and showed respect. You pulled your weight and you stayed in line. Otherwise, life was not fun.

Dad was usually off working at Cushman Motors, which supplied golf carts to all the sunny golf courses of California. He worked at that company faithfully for forty-five years raising his family of twelve kids. My mom went to work outside the home when the youngest, Brendan, started school. Then she started two businesses and went back to get her college degree, which she completed when she was seventy-two years old.

I respected and appreciated my mom. She always said that the best gift a child can have is an intelligent mother. She wanted us to be able to stand on our own and be productive. She wanted us to get our education and be independent. She wasn't easy but she was smart when it came to raising kids, and I benefited from that.

With so many kids at home, I was ready to head out on my own as soon as possible. At nineteen, I fell in love and moved to Alaska. It had all sounded so romantic and amazing. An adventure in the last frontier with an adventurer! Instead, I ended up freezing. I lasted less than a year in the tundra and then headed towards Seattle.

My visit to Seattle lasted for eight years, where I worked as a surveyor on a construction crew out in the wilds of the North. I didn't want to be a secretary, so I picked a male-dominated field. In the 1970s a woman on a survey crew was rare. There wasn't a lot of support or respect for woman swinging a machete in the forests of

Washington State. I did, however, learn to pee behind a bush, and that experience would later serve me well in the world of ultramarathons.

I remember being at a company party and one of the crew chiefs on the survey crew came up to me and commented, "My wife hates you."

I replied indignantly, "I have never met your wife!"

He said, "It doesn't matter, you are on my crew. As far as she is concerned, that is a reason to dislike you."

I was so shocked. I thought women would support one another. All I wanted was to better myself, but I had to battle the resentment of other women.

When I was twenty-four years old, I met the man of my dreams. He was so gorgeous, so tall, and beautiful that I couldn't even speak when I was introduced to him. I was head-over-heels and a short time later I found out I was pregnant. Shortly after that, he left and my heart was shattered. It was Christmas week, and I tried to prepare myself to break the news to my parents.

On Christmas Eve I went to a grocery store feeling lonely and very pregnant. I bought a half-dead fern plant because I felt sorry for it. Half the leaves fell off on the car ride home. I brought the plant into the house and picked up the phone to call my sister Karen. When I heard her voice, I began to sob. I felt like the weight of the world was on my shoulders. "It is Christmas Eve and it's just me and a dying fern!" I blubbered. "Mom and Dad are going to kill me!"

I have heard it said that during your life you can expect to have ten defining moments that shape and change the course of your life. My first defining moment was on May 23, 1981, when I first laid eyes on my beautiful son, Devin Hannegan.

I grew up on the day Devin was born. Life was giving me a new unexpected start and a chance to prove myself. I wanted to be worthy of this baby. Mary Jane flew in with all her glory, proud to be a grandmother, but also challenging me to be strong in the face of single parenthood. She marched into my house and wanted to know how I planned to support myself and Devin. She wasn't into holding hands and consoling me over my unfortunate situation of an unexpected pregnancy. She wanted to know how I was going to figure it all out, support this baby, and be self-sufficient. I was MJ's child and I wasn't permitted to miss a beat. I found a wonderful woman to watch Devin during the day, and I worked two jobs to adequately support my son.

My sister Colleen was a huge support during my entire pregnancy and beyond, moving up to Seattle to stay with me. She was my sister, my best friend, and my confidante.

An unmarried woman with a newborn back in the '80s was still taboo. People looked down on me as if I were a loser, not to mention that I was broke and struggling. But I had my ray of sunshine. That adorable baby boy filled me with such immense joy that it washed away all fear. I stood taller knowing I had been given a gift and a new mission. It was uncharted territory and a whole new adventure. I embraced the challenge, but carving out a new life wasn't easy. When a better job opportunity opened up in Las Vegas, I grabbed it. It was closer to my family in Southern California, and I was ready for a change.

I was working and attending UNLV when nine-year-old Devin and I met Bob Sheridan. He was kind and funny and wonderful. Bob was the steadfast love and support I was looking for. After a whirlwind courtship, Bob adopted Devin, whom he loved as his own, and for the next eighteen years we were together raising our family. Bailey, my adorable first daughter, came along in 1990. Sweet baby Taylor followed fifteen months later. The years I spent as a wife and mother turned out to be one of the greatest adventures of my life. I loved every single moment.

Inevitably, the kids grew up and began making plans to attend college themselves. I was facing another major chapter. My life at home with my children was ending. Bob and I were headed in separate directions. It was no one's fault.

How could I make this transition smoothly? How could I overcome the tough challenges ahead, especially with a doctor in my head telling me over and over that I was too old? I was planning on leaving my home of eighteen years because my husband and I couldn't find a compromise, and it was either leave or surrender. I had to dig deep and stand on my own two feet and tap into some of MJ's strength and self-sufficient lessons of my youth.

My overwhelming thoughts focused on freedom. I wanted peace so I could think. I'd been working through my emotions by running. I found serenity on nature trails. I found quiet and peace out in the wilds of nature. I decided that I had no desire for another relationship. All I wanted was complete and utter freedom. Those wonderful years being a full-time mother nurturing and caring for my children were gone and they weren't coming back. I was directionless except for the call of adventure. In my mind I was a total misfit who no longer fit into the confines of my community. I was in confusion and frustrated, and then I asked myself, What am I gonna do about it?

After the shock of the office visit with evil doctor dream-stealer, I got to work. Back on the Internet, I printed out instructions on pool running exercises. I took off the boot, looked at my poor swollen ankle, and stepped into the pool. Putting a floatie around my waist, I did what the instructions said: Get to the deep end of the pool without your feet touching and run in place.

Following the instructions, I ran in the water as hard as I could for two minutes then rested for thirty seconds then hit it again. The resistance from the water made the workout difficult. For weeks I hit the water working out my frustration and anger at being told I couldn't run the marathon. After each session, I had to drag myself up the pool ladder with shaky muscles sapped of every ounce of energy. My anger at Dr. Mean propelled me forward. Every time I hesitated to get back into the pool, I thought about that doc. I couldn't let him win.

I wanted freedom from the stupid boot and freedom from the opinions of the doctor and freedom from my own negative thoughts. If I was never going to be able to run effectively, my life seemed meaningless. I was on a mission to kick ass at this marathon.

In my logbook I added all the pool workouts as journal entries. It was like money in the bank. I built on that mental bank account. Six weeks pounding it out in the pool and taking care to keep the weight off my ankle came to an end. I made no attempt to go back for a checkup to the doctor because his advice was worthless to me. I put the boot aside and replaced it with my running shoe. First time back onto the streets for a run, I was overjoyed at not being out of breath or exhausted. I supposed I should have gone in for an x-ray, but the absence of pain in my ankle was good enough for me.

In the blink of an eye, it was marathon race day. I felt like a champion before I ever took a step. In my mind, I had already beat the odds.

My oldest sister, Kathy, lived near Washington, D.C., and I talked her and my daughter Bailey into running the 10K while Kylie and I ran the marathon. At the hotel, the morning of the race, my stomach was upset and I suddenly felt like I was completely unprepared. I went from feeling confident to max stress at the thought of possible failure. I forced myself to think it's gonna be a party, we're gonna have fun!

My brother-in-law, Mike Byron, Kathy's husband, was a three-star general in the Marines. He had been a talented athlete, running fast marathons under three hours. He stood near us at the start line as we were preparing to begin the race. He looked over at me and said, "What time are you shooting for in the marathon today?"

I didn't think I heard him correctly, so I repeated his question: "What time am I shooting for? I am shooting for survival, are you kidding!?! Time means nothing. I'm gonna survive this thing." Everyone around us laughed.

Thousands of spectators and 20,000 runners were gathering at the race start. The excitement and revelry filled the air. I was so proud to have a bib number pinned to my T-shirt and to be one of the athletes. Kylie and I had matching running shirts and were jumping up and down like kids. Bailey and Kathy were happily hugging us and getting ready to go to their 10K area.

I figured odds were that there were slower people than me out there. At least I hoped so! It would make me feel better not to be last. But then, I had to think that through. Isn't last better than not starting? Isn't last better than not finishing? The gun went off and we were moving within the wave of runners.

Kylie said, "Okay, let's pretend we're running in the mall." After a couple of miles she said, "Let's pretend that we're running on a deserted island." We laughed and continued to fantasize about different exotic scenarios as we ran along. Kylie and I laughed and partied our way through the marathon. We stopped to dance at all the bands, we messed around, we waved to the spectators, and thanked the Marines, who were handing out water to the runners.

Kylie kept her promise. It was FUN! It was so refreshing not to have the pressure of time. I don't think I could have taken that added pressure during that difficult transition in my live. I had enough pressure in my home life. I was lacking in confidence and self-esteem. I needed a high FUN factor to get through the race.

At the 18-mile mark, I began feeling super exhausted. It was my first un-FUN moment. I was starting to feel like a zombie. Doubt surfaced in my mind. I told Kylie that my legs felt like wet noodles.

Kylie replied, "C'mon, we're going to be so happy when we get our medals! Let's keep going."

At 20 miles we came up a hill and looked down at what appeared to be a battlefield. A lot of runners were lying on the side of the road trying to stretch out sore hamstrings and muscles. A lot of runners were now walking or sitting. As Kylie and I ran past them, I realized that I wasn't going to be the last.

Finally, in the distance, I could see Kathy waiting so patiently at the finish line with Bailey. They were cheering and waving their arms. Time meant nothing to me. I knew speed was not my gift and my goal was FUN! I put my arms up in the air, and Kylie and I ran across that finish line. I felt like I had conquered the world. Then, amidst all the clapping and cheers, a question lit up inside my brain:

I wonder how far I can run.

Mike, my brother-in-law, walked over to me and Kylie. He looked at his watch and said, "Six hours? What were you two doing out there?"

Kylie and I looked at each other, laughed, and answered simultaneously, "Having FUN!" I was beaming.

The next week I attached a picture of me crossing the finish line to "Pool running guidelines for stress fractures," and I mailed that to Dr. Mean with a note that read:

Dear Doc,

You may remember me from March. I had a stress fracture and you told me I was too old to run.

Here is a picture of me crossing the finish line at the Marine Corps Marathon in Washington, D.C. I used pool running techniques to train while my ankle healed. Enclosed is a hand-out to give any patients that come to you with a stress fracture and want to continue to stay in shape. They can keep training and stay healthy physically and mentally as they heal.

Age is a gift and an advantage when running. Never listen to anyone who doesn't understand or support your dream and your purpose.

Remember me when your next patient walks through that door.

Sincerely,
Molly

Of course, I never heard back from the doc.

CHAPTER 5

Calico Ghost Town

"Let us step into the night and pursue that flighty temptress adventure."

—J.K. Rowling, *Harry Potter and the Half-Blood Prince*

I WONDER HOW far I can run? I had no idea why that thought kept popping into my head.

I had read an article in a magazine about ultramarathons and was fascinated to discover that there are races much further than 26.2 miles. The magazine described the non-stop race Western States 100, in Northern California, one of the first ultramarathons in the country. There are aid stations in remote locations throughout the race where the runners stop to fill their water bottles and get nutrition from the volunteers supporting them day and night. The runners have to get to the aid stations in a certain amount of time, according to race regulations, or they get pulled off the course and disqualified. A typical time to finish a 100-mile race is thirty hours, although I was reading that fast runners finish a lot sooner depending upon how difficult the course is. I already knew that speed was not my gift. I simply wanted to go run distance. The thought persisted and burned inside me. I couldn't stop thinking about it. I wanted to test myself and experiment.

The distance races caught my attention and fascinated me. In my mind it was a grand adventure of epic proportions. How wild to be running free all through the night in remote and serene sections of the forest that few people had traveled much less run! I pictured running along tree-covered paths, next to river beds and lakes. I wondered what type of person ran these races. I spent hours looking up ultramarathons around the world, reading descriptions about courses and checking out the elevation gain and descent, the race regulations, and pictures of the trails. Could I do that?

That first D.C. marathon changed how I perceived myself. It was the first time in my life I had felt athletic. My dad had taught me body surfing techniques in the ocean when I was younger, but that was about it. I noticed that training for that marathon had toned my muscles. I suddenly had calf muscles on my thin legs. I lost body fat. I gained stamina. My confidence was increasing. I was stronger. Warrior Goddess.

I found a small ultra marathon race called Calico Trail Run. The event offered a 50-mile distance, but that seemed impossible to me. It also offered a 50K distance (31 miles), which intrigued me because it wasn't much further than the D.C. marathon. I could wrap my head around the idea of running a little further. It might be a little more added fun . . . right? A bonus for choosing this event was that the race was just two hours from my house, and I had never been to the area outside of Barstow in the Calico Mountains. After visiting the website 500 times, uncertain about my decision and trying not to think of all the reasons I should or shouldn't go, I registered for the race online.

At this point, with a single six-hour marathon under my belt, I wasn't exactly feeling the need to tell everybody, "I'm a badass and I'm gonna run an ultramarathon." In fact, I didn't tell anybody. I didn't tell my friends that I signed up for this new race. I didn't tell my family. Well, I did tell my husband. When I said I was going to run a race at Calico, he raised his eyebrows and commented dismissively, "Hmmm, okay." I don't know what he thought, but I was glad he didn't say anything negative. We were slowly drifting apart and our lives had become separated. We were both trying to understand how to steer towards a peaceful shore when the waves were overturning our boat.

Mentally, I was not strong enough to take any criticism at that point. I had too many whirling emotions of inadequacy. Any negative comments would have crushed me.

I didn't want people saying, "You're doing what?! That's the dumbest thing ever. You'll never make it. How stupid!" I simply couldn't take the negative so I kept silent.

If I was going to fail, I wanted to do so alone without the scrutiny of others. So I signed up for the 50K (31 mile) race, studied the Internet to see what I could learn about distance running, and I increased my miles. I quickly learned that in 2006, there was not a lot on the Internet about ultramarathons.

In the interim, I signed up for a 20-mile race up in Lake Tahoe and was making a big trip out of it and pushing family and friends to go. I encouraged my sister Colleen and my daughters Bailey and Taylor to come and bring their friends for the 10K (6.2 miles). I had co-workers who were doing the half-marathon, and my dear friends Dan and Ellen from Seattle were joining us, too. We were all going to get together for a giant weekend party and run. FUN!

Up in Lake Tahoe getting ready for my 20-mile run, I sat on my hotel room bed with papers on ultramarathons piled around me, my eyes glued to the stories of trail running. Taylor informed me that she was missing her bib number for her morning 10K, so I departed for the hotel registration to retrieve it. As I was running along the hallway, I turned, and bumped into this big, tall guy right outside the race headquarters. He reached out a hand to steady me so I wouldn't fall on my face.

He smiled. "Hi! What race are you running?"

"I am running the 20-miler," I said, so proud of myself. "Yep! Twenty big miles!"

He looked at me quietly with a friendly smile, perfect white teeth, and a silver goatee. Holding out his hand for me to shake, he said, "I'm Bill. I'm here for the triple marathon."

"You are?" He was preparing to run 72 miles. Suddenly my 20 miles seem wimpy. Then I noticed that his T-shirt read "Western States—100 miles in one day," and that he was wearing the famous Western States buckle on his belt, symbolizing his completion of the seemingly impossible.

"You're an ultramarathoner?" I asked, super-pleased to finally meet someone who ran distance. "Oh man, I gotta talk to you! I have a million questions."

He laughed and said, "Fire away. I'm waiting for my crew to come in, but they aren't arriving until later tonight so I'm around until then. You're welcome to ask any questions you'd like."

"Oh my gosh, where do I start? I am registered for my first ultramarathon." My words were rushing out: "You know what, my whole group is meeting for dinner. My family, my friends, everybody is coming to dinner, about ten of us. Do you want to meet us for dinner? You eat and I'll talk!"

Bill was so gracious meeting my friends and family, which turned out to be about twenty people. I drilled him about ultrarunning. I was surprised to learn that he was an anti-aging research scientist and his biotech facility was in Reno. He was making his own electrolyte tablets for running. He had completed over 100 ultramarathons and was a wealth of knowledge. He had received the Grand Slam of Ultrarunning award, completing some of the toughest footraces in the country in one summer. On top of that he received the inventor of the year award in the United States for his science research. He was remarkable, and everyone at the table was intently listening to him talk about the latest anti-aging research in addition to his adventures in endurance running. It was one of the most interesting conversations I have ever experienced.

Bill would eventually became a dear friend. He was so knowledgeable about how to take care of your body during long distance runs. He gave me tips on how a runner keeps energy levels up during a race through good nutrition. He discussed the amount of water a runner needs to drink in order to keep from getting dehydrated.

I ran the 20-mile race at Lake Tahoe with Bill's inspirational thoughts and helpful tips bouncing around in my brain. I was awed by the beautiful scenery as I proudly completed my second race. I was still slow. I had to walk at times, but I beat the deadline. Nevertheless, Calico would be 11 more miles. Was I capable?

Calico is an old mining community off I-15 about 20 miles north of Barstow. When I arrived all by myself in my little car, I was stunned at the remoteness of the setting. The only signs of civilization were a truck stop and a rundown lodging facility that reminded me of the Bates Motel in the movie Psycho. I sat in the car and stared at my new surroundings, overwhelmed with feelings of fear and insecurity. I was glad I hadn't told anyone about this venture, because that left open the option of returning to my safe, secure home in Las Vegas. After sitting motionless for the longest time, I compelled my body to exit the vehicle and walk into the lobby. Maybe this is just a scary dream, I thought to myself.

I dumped my stuff in the no-frills room and walked over to the truck stop restaurant. When I walked in the door, twenty pairs of trucker eyes turned and stared at me ... scary trucker eyes. It creeped me out as I scanned the room for anyone who looked like Anthony Perkins.

After hurriedly eating a yucky meal, I drove up the street to the community center, which housed the packet pick-up area for the race. Several runners were lined up, picking up their race T-shirts and bibs. My mood was lifted by the buzz of energy and the fact that other people were doing the same thing as me. Maybe I hadn't lost my mind after all.

I felt out of place because it was such a strange world. I was in my still, stealth mode. I quietly grabbed my stuff, shuffled out to my car, and got back to the quiet of my ratty motel room. I didn't want to explain myself or be social with anyone. I just wanted to get out on the trails in the morning. I was glad I hadn't told anyone about the venture, but I was unsettled and nervous to go it alone. Yet, deep inside was my internal thrill at being there, this secret world of ultra-marathons. This is where I wanted to be. This is what I wanted to experience. It was thrilling and scary all rolled into one. My fear of attempting a trail run in the middle of nowhere along with being totally on my own somehow made me feel very much alive and in control of my own destiny. I was supposed to be doing this for some reason. I was supposed to be testing myself. I didn't exactly understand my own feelings, but I knew that I didn't want to be anywhere else but in that race.

That night, back in my hotel room I put on the news and the weather forecast informed me that a freezing cold front was moving in and temperatures were dropping below freezing.

I was glad I had come prepared with my super warm jacket, my U.S. Marine Corps beanie, and my gloves, which I laid out on the bed, but I knew this was going to be a tough way to start the race. Below freezing temps at 5:00 a.m. in the morning, out in the dark, at race start was challenging.

I got up in the morning, after a fitful night filled with sounds of Norman Bates outside my door trying to jiggle my doorknob back and forth. I dressed quickly and stuck my head out into the hallway to see if the coast was clear. I ran to my car, the frozen air striking me like a blow from a baseball bat. I slammed down the door locks before some guy dressed like his mother came rushing after me.

I could barely keep my emotions in check. Not only was I scared out of my wits because of the accommodations, I was preparing to run further than I'd ever run before . . . in the desert . . . in freezing temperatures . . . in the dark. Maybe this is what happens, I thought to myself, when people start to have nervous breakdowns. They go to ratty cheap motels after signing up for an endurance run and just crack. Maybe I'm a mad woman. Do they do strange stuff like this? I don't know, but here we go.

Seventy runners were milling around as I approached the starting area, all of them freezing, stomping around, and wondering what in the world got them out of their cozy beds. At least that's what I was wondering. Doubt crept in. I started looking around to see if there were any other mad housewives who were out there with me. There were lots of runners, but I didn't see anyone in their fifties.

I spotted one young guy who reminded me of my son Devin. He was wearing only a tank top and shorts. He was jumping around flapping his arms. I approached and asked, "Don't you have a jacket?" My motherly instincts were kicking in.

He replied, "I'm from Wisconsin, I came to this race because it's in California and California is supposed to be warm. I'm freezing my ass off!"

Suddenly I was in my element. "Look, you have time before the start of the race. You go jump in your car and drive down to the gas station. They sell sweatshirts. It's not gonna get warm anytime soon and you're going to be freezing for hours."

He didn't miss a beat as he headed for his car. Over his shoulder, he shouted, "Thanks!"

A few minutes later, I saw him back at race line-up with a sweatshirt on. He waved at me and pointed to the front of his sweatshirt, which read, "I Love Barstow."

Maybe the reason I was out there was to use my mothering skills.

I smiled to myself. I was thinking, hey, if nothing else, maybe I'm supposed to be a mother to all these runners out here. I laughed out loud.

Suddenly the gun went off and I began to run. I had my little headlamp, which threw out a steady beam in front of me. I had my lightweight backpack with a hydration pack to hold 50 ounces of water. I was ready to make a day of it out in the wild open spaces surrounding Calico Ghost Town.

I was scared, excited, freaked and happy. All those amazing feelings were flowing through me simultaneously. How else could I experience such emotions? I had a huge smile on my face that I could not wipe off.

I followed along with the runners and I kept saying to myself, "Molly, don't look at anybody else. Don't you care what anyone else is doing. Just do your thing. Even if you're the very last person, and you have to drag yourself across the finish line, who cares, Molly? This is your time now."

My heart was pounding out of my chest. I was so . . . alive. The sun came up and the surrounding desert came to life as well. The mountains were a dazzling array of purple and orange. The trail was gorgeous. It was freezing, but I didn't care. I got to the first aid station, and I heard a happy volunteer say, "Welcome, you just made it six miles. You are doing awesome." I looked around and realized she was talking to me.

I was free. The trails were so beautiful. Dry, dusty trails weaved back into the red canyons. I ran. My feet felt light as my head and heart soaked up the beauty. After miles, even when the fatigue crept in, I still had the euphoria of being in a place of infinite happiness.

I ran through the canyons up and down dry creek beds. Cactus and Mesquite trees lined my path. On difficult ascents, I power-walked up, then ran down the other side, moving through space. I had entered the secret world of trail running, and my heart was filled with joy.

Finally after seven hours, I was approaching the finish line. The mountainous terrain had been difficult and challenging for me. My first marathon had taken me six hours. Here I was, an hour later, finishing a 31-miler on a much tougher course. I was so proud of myself.

The Warrior Goddess was flying along the trail. What a badass! Only a quarter mile to go. I could see volunteers at the finish line cheering for runners. Cheering for me! Suddenly my toe snagged a sharp pile of rocks. I crashed down and split both of my knees open. Blood flowed down my legs. It was such a shock that I sat there for a minute checking the damage. I was covered in sweat, dirt and blood. I was so thankful that it looked worse than it really was. I picked myself up and did Warrior Goddess ego check. I looked like Norman Bates had stabbed me through the shower curtain and dragged my body through the desert.

I crossed the finish line with my USMC beanie on, both my knees streaming blood, and a big smile on my face. A spectator yelled," Are you a Marine?" I shouted back, waving, "Nope. But I feel like one right now!"

Everyone laughed and congratulated me as I jumped over the finish line with a ridiculous grin on my face. Medics quickly patched me up with a couple of white gauze strips and tape. I walked around with my bandages of bravery, USMC hat, dirt from head to toe. I had made it 31 miles! Official badass!

Just then the announcer said, "Molly Sheridan second place, age group award."

I was stunned! The race director handed me a huge trophy, second place in my age group. It was a gorgeous, hand-painted saw-mill blade from Calico Ghost Town. I was never so proud of any accomplishment besides the birth of my kids. I was astounded that I had beat anyone. It shocked me to the core.

It was a glorious moment, holding the trophy and experiencing an overwhelming sense of confidence and accomplishment. I sat down and let my sense of wonder sink in. I wanted to run farther. I had three races under my belt: 26.2 miles, 20 miles, and 31 miles. I wondered if it was possible for me to run 100 miles.

CHAPTER 6

Rio Del Lago—100 Miles

"Mom, your hair looked great the first 50 miles. The
last 50 miles it turned into an incredible rat nest!"
—Taylor Sheridan, 15 year old crew member

"MOM, THIS IS sooooo awesome!" my sixteen-year-old daughter Bailey proclaimed as we trudged through the dark parking lot making our way to the start line where all the runners were gathering. We were bundled up in the 40-degree chill. Why she would choose "awesome," I couldn't guess.

"This is sooooo early," moaned fifteen-year-old Taylor, as she hung on my arm with her head on my shoulder. We trudged through the dark, the full moon brilliant above us, casting shadows along the foot path as we passed through the trees.

Bailey activated the voice recorder which they were supposed to use to keep track of times in and out of the aid stations. Bailey announced, "Mom makes her way to the start line." She turned to me like a seasoned news reporter: "Any last words, Mom?"

"No." I was preoccupied, my mind in turmoil, and I was simply in no mood to be chatty.

Bailey continued in her deadpan monotone voice. "What exactly are you thinking at this great moment, Mom? Any words at all, Mom . . . anything?"

"No," I snapped, zoned out in my own world, wondering what possessed me to undertake such a feat without sufficient training. I should have had several more months of preparation. My body was tense with anxiety. I began to bite my lip, my head down, watching the ground as we walked.

"Oh, my gawd!" Taylor suddenly woke up, her long blonde hair flipping to the side as she glanced to Bailey. "She's freaked out! Mom is freaking! Hahahaha. This is sooooo wild!"

Wild? I glared at them. Yes, I conceded to myself, this is wild and, yes, I'm freaked. I continued the slow march to the start line, my thoughts unfocused. I felt like I was moving in a dream, a sort of out-of-body experience, my mind curiously detached. Through the dense trees, I could see the runners gathering. The hum of voices and the bright lights of the start line carried out into the surrounding dark forest paths. Taylor bounded ahead, a wired teenager unused to being up at the crack of dawn. I followed her to the large group of race participants gathered around a heat lamp near the trailhead, stomping around trying to stay warm. Their voices seemed reassuring for a brief moment.

Well, here I am, I told myself quietly. I looked around, peering at the check-in table. Runners were pinning on their numbers. Several runners were stretching. I felt like an outsider. I didn't belong with these athletes. My old familiar thoughts played like a broken record in my mind. I immediately tried to find women my age, anyone who looked at least fifty, so I wouldn't feel so out of place. Fifty years old and my first 100-mile endurance run. Why did everyone look so young? Stop it, Molly, I internally admonished myself. Get a grip. It's too late now. You are committed . . . or, indeed, you should be committed. Yet, completing the distance in under thirty hours seemed utterly impossible.

Life passes so quickly then goes into warp speed after fifty. I wanted to grab onto all that life had to offer. Now that I had accomplished my long-term goal of having children and raising a family, I needed to achieve personal goals. I had been on a high that year after running 31 miles in Calico and two other races, but this was three times as far.

I had also been trying to handle my earth-shattering divorce. I tried meditation, sitting on a mat to find my peace and serenity, but I was a complete failure. Running was the only thing that quieted my mind and freed my heart. Sometimes I would listen to music while running, sometimes I would listen to nothing. Running in nature was my quiet meditation, which produced incredible moments that were deeply spiritual. On days that I couldn't keep the tears at bay, running released the sadness. Moving through life's transitions was a rough business for me. The end of my relationship with my husband had taken a toll. I picked the 100-mile race simply because it seemed impossible. And I was stubborn enough to want to test the impossible. Others had lots of talent and speed, but could I do it? The idea was bigger than me, but I found myself drawn to that mysterious question: how far can I go?

I had been told that every runner has a better chance of finishing a 100-mile ultramarathon if they have a crew to support them. The crew supplies the runner with food and extra clothing, and offers encouragement through the long hours of the night and into the second day.

I suggested to Bailey and Taylor (Bay and Tay) that they accompany me on my adventure and act as my crew. Bay was in immediately. No questions asked. No hesitation. Tay had to be convinced that there would be some level of fun. (Who did that sound like?) The first obstacle was convincing her to get up at 4:00 a.m. I now questioned the wisdom of encouraging my youngest to step out of her comfort zone of boys, parties, and makeup, and to instead embrace the outdoors with all its dirt, bugs, and snakes.

I scanned the crowd for my buddy Bill. Reassurance would be a great relief right about now. Our friendship had continued over the last year, but it was rare that I saw him. Mostly we sent each other emails with opinions on endurance running. He was busy traveling all over the world giving lectures on his research on telomeres and anti-aging. He wasn't running today, but was here to assist the race director and to run one of the aid stations.

I looked over at Tay and Bay, who now resembled fireflies dancing around the race start area . . . teenage hyper-happiness. Their matching hot pink "Molly's Crew" T-shirts were like neon beams in the crowd. A young, pretty, twenty-something athlete leaned toward me and asked, "Who's Molly?" I ignored the question.

I spotted Buddy Bill as he sauntered toward me. Tall and lanky, Bill always stands out in a crowd. His lean frame is a testament to years of successful endurance races. With a big grin on his face, he gave me a bear hug and wished me luck. I mentally thanked him for not giving me any last words of advice. I loved the fact that my dear friend wasn't overly protective, although little did he realize at that very moment I had frantic visions of leaping into his arms and begging and pleading for him to take me back to the car. My mental fog had lifted, leaving a sinking terror in its wake. I felt sick, my legs hurt, no, everything hurt, and I had a migraine. I wanted to shriek, "I quit!" when I hadn't even started. Instead, I looked up into his calm face and said quietly, "Thanks, Bill." I felt better with him near, my mentor and friend whom I called Buddy with great affection.

The little happiness and excitement I possessed was melting into irritation and crankiness as my stress level spiked. Molly, what were you thinking? I yelled silently to myself, but it was too late. I spotted Georganna, whom I had met the previous day at the race meeting. She was adorable and petite and one of the few runners near my age. She seemed confident and composed, and we hugged and wished each other luck.

The race director called out, "Five minutes to start!" My heart dropped into a pit. I lined up with the other runners. Bay and Tay were giddy with excitement, jumping up and down while holding hands, dancing with glee. I reminded them, "Girls, don't forget to record my times in and out of the aid stations." My mothering instincts came back to me suddenly. "Check in with Bill so he knows where you are for the next thirty hours. Also, DO NOT be at the first aid station. No crew is allowed there!"

"We know. Don't worry, Mom. Have fun!"

The race director yelled, "Good luck, runners!"

Bay and Tay raced over for a last hug, screaming and shrieking in the frenzy and excitement of the moment. Oh, my God, I thought, I have Paris Hilton and Nicole Richie for a crew. "Bye, Mom," they yelled in unison. "See you at the aid stations." Bay screamed, "Whoot whoot!"

A voice in a microphone boomed, "10, 9, 8, 7, 6." Shit, I thought to myself. Shit, shit . . . shit. Off I ran into the dark woods, immersed in a sea of runners . . . onward toward 100 miles.

Nerves are a funny thing. They can wind you into a knot with guts twisted and shoulders tight. It's no way to run. As I jogged out along the dark trail, I was hyperventilating and hunched over like an old woman. I had to get a grip. Deep breaths, long deep breaths. I needed to slow my pace. The worst thing for me at that early moment would be to run a faster pace than I had planned and burn myself out early. It was difficult to resist the urge to keep up with the crowd of athletes, but I didn't want to be last. Gradually I slowed and forced myself to follow my plan. I thought about Bailey and Taylor at the start, yelling and clapping with the other spectators. Their excitement carried me, and I found myself smiling at the absurdity of the moment. I was also exhilarated. I wanted this! I wanted the challenge. I wanted to experience every moment of this race. Aid stations stocked with food and drink were spread out every five or six miles through the forest. My goal was to spend less than two minutes at each aid station. In a 100-mile race with fourteen aid stations available, it is easy to rack up hours of wasted time hanging out too long at the table of food and drink while chatting with volunteers.

I silently repeated my mantra: move through space . . . move through space. I felt peaceful.

Soon I saw the aid station through the trees. The race director had given strict instructions that no crew members could be at Twin Rocks, the first aid station. They did not want a traffic jam of crew driving frantically to the first aid station so early in the race. Oh, no! Two bright pink T-shirts. There they were, the renegade teenagers, breaking the rules. I saw them behind a tree, trying to be inconspicuous with their Molly Crew T-shirts and, I could scarcely believe my eyes, pompoms. Their little cheery faces were mouthing the words, "HI, MOM . . . SURPRISE!"

I wondered if a runner could get disqualified for an unruly crew. Then I saw Bill walk up behind them with a big smile on his face, and I knew he was behind the rule breaking. Bill, it turned out, was actually the aid station captain for Twin Rocks. I waved and laughed and continued on. I was glad that at least they showed up for one aid station even though I didn't need them yet and they weren't supposed to be there. Ha! This was going to be interesting.

The morning continued on with a gorgeous sunrise and partly cloudy skies. I ran along Folsom Lake, passing more aid stations with cool names like Horseshoe Bar and Rattlesnake. Sometimes I would chat with a runner for a minute or two, but mostly I kept to myself and the calming rhythm of my shoes tapping along the trail. I stopped on a rocky ridge above the lake and took a few deep breaths. What a gorgeous place. I wanted to enjoy the journey. My goal was to finish. I had no pressure about trying to place or win. My competition was with myself. Speed was never my gift. In training I always tried to keep up a decent pace, but I knew my limitations. Of course, I knew less about my limitations in a 100-mile distance since the farthest distance I had run during training (or ever) was 50 miles. Thankfully, Bay and Tay continued to faithfully show up at the aid stations. It was fun and reassuring to see them as I came in for food and water. We were all working on a quick system whereby I handed off my water bottle for them to fill, and they supplied me with additional food, chips, pretzels, and gel (small foil packets of concentrated nutrition) to stick into my pack. It looked like they were having fun and I was relieved whenever I saw them, because it meant that they had found the different checkpoints and I didn't have to worry that they were lost. I also noticed that Bay was actually using the voice recorder as I ran into the aid stations. That was going to be so helpful to me after the race so I could evaluate my performance at various stages and adjust for the future.

Late in the day I was approaching the 50-mile mark, where I was now permitted by race regulations to pick up a pacer. Pacers help keep a runner moving on the lonely forest trails. With nightfall approaching, I was looking forward to a pacer who could run in front of me and shine extra light on the trail. Fatigue was taking a toll on my body both physically and mentally. I was relieved at the thought that my pacer would assume responsibility for navigating obstacles and, more importantly, avoiding becoming lost—one of my greatest fears. Terra joined me, and I loved the company.

I was exhausted and filthy from running all day. I had run 50 miles in twelve hours on difficult trails that rolled up and down through the mountains. Terra was chatting about men, which was a good thing because she kept my attention away from the task at hand. I didn't want to think about the fact that I had 50 more miles to go. I enjoyed hearing her views on men so I could escape the focus of my physical anguish. Hot, dirty, and dusty, I needed comic relief.

"So," Terra continued in her upbeat tone, "after my first husband beat me up and broke my leg, I realized that I was in an unhealthy relationship!"

"No way!?!" I exclaimed. That caught my attention. "Seriously, Terra, you look like you just stepped out of a fashion magazine." I trudged up a mountain of rocks and cactus, my feet sore from pebbles and grit.

"I was pretty wild," she continued. "I once decked a guy in a bar."

"Really?" My astonishment was palpable. I couldn't believe my adorable girlfriend, with her sweet husband and perfect kids, was once a bar brawler!

Run together with anyone on a long trail race, and you will hear the most interesting life histories. Maybe it's the endorphins popping or energy flowing, but one way or another, bonding with your pacer is common. Either that or you are ready to strangle them after hours of exhaustion.

"It was pretty bad," she reflected as she picked up rocks on the trail and tossed them to the side.

"Excuse me for interrupting, Terra, but why are you moving the rocks on the trail?"

"For the other runners behind us," she chirped.

There aren't many of those, I thought. Terra was the most kind, mothering, and considerate person I knew. "Don't you think more rocks are going to fall onto this course? You can't get all of them."

"Well, hopefully, that will happen after the race," she said as she continued to run ahead of me and clear the course like she was tidying up her house.

Rounding another corner, we came upon the carcass of a large deer. It was sprawled on top of our trail, blood and guts spilled all around. I halted in amazement. The deer's neck was snapped back, and the bones and rib cage were pointed upwards, red, bloody, and gory.

Terra examined it closely. "Molly, this happened a short time ago. It's either a bear or a mountain lion that attacked this deer. We need to run hard and get away from here as soon as possible," she calmly warned.

"Holy Crap!" was all I could say. I nervously looked behind me, around me, and back behind me again. Terra took off and I speeded up behind her.

"My uncle is a hunter," she yelled back to me as she ran. "He taught me how wild animals, like bears and mountain lions, kill their prey." She flew along at a clip. Her strides were longer and faster. I think that was a mountain lion from the look of it," she commented.

"Okay, okay, enough of the details," I shouted, my fear and worry mounting. Suddenly I was not tired anymore and my pace was approaching Olympic speeds.

"I am hoping that whatever was eating that deer isn't hungry anymore," Terra said.

"Let's keep moving! I am totally freaked out now!" I flashed another look behind me, wondering what I would do if indeed the big cat was nearby and ready to pounce.

"If it wanted to attack you," she continued to lecture as if she were a college professor, "you would never know it until it was on you. They are extremely stealth."

"Terra! Geezuz! Too much information."

As we approached No Hands Bridge at the thirty-mile mark, I was never so happy to hit an aid station. The cougar/bear/mountain lion out there feasting on deer hadn't attacked, and my pace was steady. I spotted Bay and Tay, who were pulling food out of an ice chest. I also noticed two teenage boys helping them. Hmmm. My crew had suddenly doubled in size.

I didn't have time to take down names and numbers. Taylor said, "That's my mom!" as I quickly waved and gathered my supplies.

"Mom, you are really looking good and you are ahead of schedule!" Bailey said.

I didn't mention to them that I was running my ass off to keep from being eaten. Both girls gave me a big hug, and I was so glad that they seemed to be working conscientiously. In fact, I was amazed that they were rushing to send me off. Wow, they were being so efficient! I headed down the trail and turned back to wave, but I could see that the boys had already recaptured their attention. Oh well, I thought, at least they were meeting new friends.

At 70 miles I pulled on a pair of headphones and pretended I was dancing. I love to dance. It's amazing how you can dance for hours and not be tired. I started listening to African women drumming music that I had gotten from my sister Colleen. It was incredible and I felt renewed.

At the 75-mile mark, however, I hit a wall. I felt like my veins were full of lead. Gravity sucked the energy right out of me. I walked for a while to conserve energy, eat, and get a renewed second wind. In this case it was like a tenth wind because I was in a continuing cycle of energy and exhaustion. One moment I felt great as I danced along, followed by a desire to simply lie down. Then I'd have a bite to eat, walk a little, and feel rejuvenated. Then exhaustion would take over. It was a continuous cycle that kept changing, but no matter how tired I got, I could move past it by walking and eating and getting my head focused on moving through space. It was a constant mind over matter battle.

I looked at my GPS and realized that I was approaching the 80-mile mark. I could see the lights at the aid station and there, in the distance, was my Taylor, who had spotted me and was jumping up and down.

Wow, I thought, she is so proud and excited for me! She was waving her arms and swaying back and forth in anticipation of my arrival. I was the Warrior Goddess. Wonder Mom. That was me. My heart swelled with pride at the example I was setting for my girls. I might even be voted Mother of the Year for Outstanding Achievement! I was so exhausted and dirty that I wanted to walk, but I decided to run into the aid station to show my kids that I was their superhero. Taylor was clapping now and running up to meet me. Her face was pure joy. I realized that I had become the most important adult symbol in her life . . . The Most Incredible Mother Ever!

"Mom!" Taylor embraced me. "Mom! The guys here are so HOT!" I stopped in my tracks and stared at my daughter. "Oh, my gawd, Mom!" She continued to jump around. "I will crew for you anytime! These guys are unbelievable!" My Mother of the Year vision was shattered. "Mom, look at the six-pack on that guy with his shirt off!"

Bailey joined in. "These guys are running with their shirts off, Mom. Look at him!" I was sweaty, dirty, grimy, and now, cranky. I had just completed 80 miles through a forest at night, and my daughters were acting as if I'd just returned from the grocery store. They weren't even looking at me. Instead, they took turns pointing excitedly at one boy after another. I didn't know whether I should scream in anger, break down sobbing, or simply drop dead right then and there. I wondered how long it would take them to notice my corpse strewn across the trail. "Can I have some water?" I croaked.

Taylor grabbed my water bottle. "Oh, do you need water?" she continued as she peered behind me to see if there were any shirtless guys she might have missed.

"Yes, water," I gasped.

Bay and Tay ran over to the aid station table as I adjusted my headlamp and regrouped. "Here ya go, Mom!" announced Bay as she handed me the bottle.

I put the spout to my lips to take a drink, but the lid came off, spilling the entire contents down my shirt.

"Oops, sorry, Mom! Forgot to screw the cap back on!" Bay said as Taylor tapped her on the back.

"There he is!" Tay whispered. "The Greek god!" pointing to a young runner.

"Okay, girls, glad you are having fun. Your dead tired and miserable mother is leaving now." I tried to remind myself that teenagers are on another planet. I waved to them. "Don't worry about me! Off to get devoured by some wild animal," I shouted.

"Hahahaha, Mom, you are so funny! See you at the next aid station!" They both laughed, waved, and ran for the car.

A short while later things began to unravel. I was informed at mile 85 that I was behind and needed to pick up the pace in order to make the cutoff time of thirty hours. I hated that news. Pick up the pace? I was dragging.

Bill jumped in to pace me, which was a relief. I needed his experience and his quiet. He knew at this point that I was just trying to pull it together and dig deep. Putting one foot in front of the other was a challenge. Everything in me was screaming to stop. My feet hurt and my legs ached. I felt like I had been summiting Everest. Bill didn't say a word and I was grateful because I wanted someone to yell at. If he said anything like, "How are you feeling?" or "Are you doing okay?" I would have let loose a hurricane of frustration. Never, never ask a runner how they are doing at 85 miles. You don't want the truth and they aren't going to lie.

I zoned in on his heels and just tried to keep up. I had no idea of the time and I didn't want to know. I knew he was on top of it. I knew that he wouldn't let me get any further behind. The trail seemed endless. By now I had gone through the night and exhausted three pacers. I had spent over twenty-nine hours on my feet.

As I was running in a trance, Bill suddenly stopped, placed his hands on my shoulders, and said, "You have a mile left and your girls are waiting for you just ahead. Well done!"

My heart leapt in my chest. I suddenly felt elated! My tiredness was replaced by pure joy. Then Bay and Tay appeared. We held hands and ran toward the finish line. Taylor looked at my puffy hands and said, "Oh wow, you have marshmallow hands, ewww!" Then we all started laughing, and crossed the line together. Bill captured the moment in a photo that I will always treasure. Success. 29:29:10. Thirty minutes to spare.

Taylor, Molly, and Bailey at the Finish line of the Rio Del Lago 100

Events after the race were a blur. I remember receiving an award for finishing the 100 miles. I also remember my friend Georganna taking photos and walking around effortlessly, although she had also run 100 miles. I remember shuffling to the car, but I don't remember anything else.

When I woke up in the hotel room the next morning, I felt paralyzed. I imagine it was similar to waking up after surviving a crushing avalanche or maybe being hit by a semi on a bike. I couldn't have felt worse if I had been thrown around the ring by a giant Sumo wrestler.

At first I couldn't move my legs. When I finally managed some motion, they were screaming at me. Taylor saw me struggling, rolled out of bed, grabbed a leg and swung me into sitting position. Just then the phone rang and she dumped me. Diving for the phone she said, "OH, my gawd, I think that's Mark!"

"Who is Mark?" I asked, hoping he was a masseuse or a chiropractor.

"He's the Greek god with the six-pack!" she whispered as she covered the phone. I stood and teetered, trying to move stiff and sore muscles. I reached out to steady myself wondering how in the world I could walk. I began to rock back and forth like I was in a full body cast. Tipping worked to move because I was using gravity instead of body parts. I downed a bunch of Ibuprofen thinking if my kidneys failed, it probably wouldn't compare to the pain in my legs; having a major organ stop functioning wouldn't be noticeable.

I plastered a fake smile on my face so I wouldn't freak out my girls (after they got off the phone and once again noticed me), and practiced walking. I started to sway like the leaning Tower of Pisa. I was so ticked that I hadn't trained harder. I knew that this was a rookie mistake, taking on 100 miles without being completely ready. I peeked out my blinds into the hotel common area. Other runners were walking! Walking around happily!

We packed up our belongings and got ready to drive home. Seven hours in the car was going to be a chore. I was tossed into the back seat. I could tell that my crew was done taking care of me. They were ready to blast home to their friends and social life.

Bailey showed me pictures she had taken of me in the back seat after the race. I was completely comatose with hair that resembled a rat's nest and dirt obscuring my face. "Thanks, Bay," I said. "I'll keep that to remind me of the glamorous part of running."

As we headed for home, Taylor pulled out pen and paper. "Okay," she said, "let's make a list of supplies we need for the next race!"

"I want a rainbow umbrella and Mom needs more snacks," Bailey chimed in.

Tay began to write furiously. I thought back to the first time I had asked Taylor to crew. She did not want to go and made faces telling me no way was she sitting out in the boonies with hillbillies. Ha!

Later on in the ride, I asked the girls for the voice recorder so I could listen to the recordings of my times in and out of the aid stations.

"Oh um, well" Bailey said as she handed me the recorder. "I'm not sure how accurate those are."

"I understand" I replied, "it's a long time crewing and I know that you may have missed some, but I just want a general idea of my time." I noticed that Bailey and Taylor both silently glanced at each other in the front seat. I hit the play button.

All I could hear was uncontrollable laughing. I sat in stunned silence as I listened to what was supposed to be my documented times in and out of the aid stations.

"I see a llama! A llammmaaaaa!"

"Bay, give it to me! It's my turn to record!"

"Cut it out, you brat, I want it."

"Stop it! I'm telling Mom!"

"I see the llama again! Look, a llama!"

Silence for a few seconds. "Mom has arrived at aid station three at approximately, around 11 a.m. . . . ish."

"Sorry, Mom, we missed the first aid stations . . . we love you!"

"Mom has arrived at another aid station. What number is this? Seven? Maybe eight. It is approximately 2:00 a.m., I think. Bay, what time is it?"

"It's 3 a.m. in the morning and we are looking for a 7-Eleven. HAHAHAHA! Party!"

"Bailey hit a trash can with the car. Bailey, you are so busted!" On and on the girls bantered. Only two recorded times for me, and even those were uncertain. I lay down in the back seat of that car. A thought popped into my head: an Xtreme sport is raising teenagers.

I had to laugh. What a wild ride and an amazing adventure. I felt like I had conquered something back there. I felt free. I felt love for my girls and joy at our victory. We came and conquered. We all experienced something that was bigger than ourselves. I was so proud of my wonderful, wacky, adorable girls. People had often said to me, "Oh brother, you have teenagers? That's tough!" Tough? No way. Teenagers are cool. Teenagers are fun. Insert them into an adventure and they will make it special.

As time goes by, I cherish the memories of that very first 100-miler more and more. Kids grow older and move on with their own lives. But memories stay. I will always remember my first 100-mile ultra-marathon at Rio Del Lago.

CHAPTER 7

Jane's 50-Mile Race

"It doesn't matter how slowly you go as long as you do not stop."

—Confucius

THE PUB WAS quiet for a Sunday afternoon. We had agreed to meet after her latest doctor's appointment, and I was anxious to get information from her in person. Jane and I had shared everything for the last twenty years of our friendship. The waitress walked up just after we slid into the booth, and we each immediately ordered a glass of white wine.

Jane had a calm expression on her face. I had always wanted her beautiful complexion, not to mention her thick and gorgeous golden blonde hair. She had been a top administrator for the school district and had just retired at the ripe age of fifty-two. Smart and savvy, she had a killer sense of humor and could easily have won More Magazine's women over forty modeling contract. We had raised our kids together and sent them off to college at the same time. We had shared our married lives and spent years vacationing together at the beach. Jane always seemed smarter and wiser than me. I loved everything about her. I dreaded the subject of our meeting.

"I have breast cancer," she said. I sat there stunned, completely unprepared for her remark. Jane was my alter-ego, my confidante, and a staunch supporter of my ultrarunning. Never a runner herself, she embraced the passion for my sake.

The cancer comment hung in the air for a few moments. The waitress brought over our wine. I took some time to gather my thoughts, took a sip, and looked over at Jane. "How bad is it?" I took a second gulp to calm my fears.

"I have three lumps, and I have to have a mastectomy," she replied matter-of-factly.

Holy shit, I wanted to scream. If I could have picked the most unlikely person to have cancer, it would have been Jane. She was super active, the picture of a strong woman—someone who loved cooking healthy meals and working out. I sat in disbelief.

"Look," Jane said matter-of-factly, "I've thought a lot about this. I'm not in any position other than to just battle it out. Plus," she paused and looked over at me, "I always wanted to see what kind of shape my head has." Then she laughed. How could she be laughing?

We talked for a long time. I tried to comfort her, but with her calm demeanor and light-hearted conversation, she ended up comforting me instead. In the weeks that followed, the rippling effect of her illness made me stop in my tracks to think about my own life and the precious time we have on this earth.

As the months passed, I watched my beautiful and healthy friend slowly go down the path of hair loss, weakness, and the pain of surgery and chemo treatments. I watched other more nurturing friends give Jane the steadfast support I seemed unable to provide. I felt guilty and inadequate as a friend. I justified my separateness from her by convincing myself that her other friends were there to give her better support than I could. I didn't think she would miss having me around. My racing schedule became an escape mechanism to free my mind from Jane's illness. Struggling at that time with my own divorce, I was overwhelmed with life's difficulties.

During a particularly difficult time, I stopped by her home to sit with her for a while. I was scheduled to depart that evening for a 50K (31 mile) race near Auburn, California. Jane was sitting in a chair, her head wrapped in a scarf. She was hunched over because she had recently had her mastectomy, and I could tell from her pale face that she was struggling with a lot of pain.

With a wry smile despite her discomfort, Jane began, "You know, I've been thinking about how similar our lives are right now."

Perplexed by this comment, I asked, "Like how?"

"Like . . ." she replied, "you are going through a divorce and I'm going through cancer. They are both trying to kill us!" She started chuckling. "Oh crap, laughing makes me hurt," she added as she held a pillow to her chest. Here she was, laughing again.

"Oh Jane, you are a scream," I said.

"No, really, Molly. Think about it. Society thinks you have done something wrong to get the curse of cancer or the curse of divorce. Everyone treats you like you have the plague." Then she continued a low laugh so as not to hurt her chest.

I looked at her and just cracked up. "You are right, Jane; we have solidarity with our personal burdens . . . we rock!!" And we both laughed. I looked over at her with love and respect. I've never witnessed a braver woman. She continued to try to make me feel good by asking all sorts of questions about my race. "Are you all set?" she continued with her weak smile. "Are you ready for the race?"

I felt guilty. I felt sad that I was departing on my own adventure, while she remained trapped in her ghastly sick body. I noticed her bracelet and asked, "Jane, can I wear your bracelet during my race? That way, you can be there and run with me every step of the way."

She smiled so big, and then unclasped the silver charm bracelet from her wrist. "Deal! Run like hell and no falling!" She and I laughed as I remembered her shock at my stories of some of my famous falls during races. The name Crash Sheridan had followed me around for quite some time. When I first started trail running, I didn't have properly fitted shoes. I later found that my shoes were slightly too large, which caused me to trip over roots and other protrusions. "Crashing" was the term we used. One particular bad fall was an ungraceful spill down a long embankment in front of a group of my fellow competitors. One guy actually clapped and called out "10!" The very next race, a runner came up alongside of me on the trail and said, "Hey, I remember you. Sheridan . . . right? Crash Sheridan. Dang, that last fall of yours was awesome!" At the end of that race someone else pointed and said, "Hi, Crash!" Thus was born my nickname.

When Jane handed me her charm bracelet, I immediately felt the energy from this small symbol circling my own wrist. I felt empowered, as if on a mission. At the same time, I was overwhelmed at Jane's illness, and the feelings of helplessness washed over me. My life was like swirling rapids of mixed emotions.

Later that night after my plane landed in Sacramento, I arrived at the hotel, tired and unusually anxious about the race. I called Jane. I didn't know why but I was extra lonely. I had flashbacks of the two of us escaping down the beach, stealing time away from our families to sip wine on the sand and watch the waves. That had been a more carefree time in our lives. I thought about our uncontrollable laughter on a million different occasions. "Jane," I said after a slight pause on the phone, "I haven't been a good friend to you. It is a horrible helpless feeling for me to see you sick. I haven't known what to do. If I could somehow transfer your cancer to myself, I would." I started sobbing. I heard her quiet crying as I continued. "I can't do anything for you, Jane, but I can run. I'm going to be running for you tomorrow." I heard her catch her breath and let out a sob, and then another. Then we were both openly weeping on the phone. After five minutes of intense heartache, I suddenly stopped and proclaimed, "Oh, my

God! This is too pitiful, and pitiful isn't tolerable. We are the saddest people on the planet and we've gotta stop! It's like a Shakespeare tragedy. Let's talk about something fun!!" We chatted for a few more minutes and promised each other that we would always be the best of friends. We ended the phone call on a positive note. I grabbed my jacket on the hotel night stand, clutched my rental car keys, and headed over to pick up my race packet.

The night was cool as I scanned the sky for clouds. It was clear and calm as the weather report had predicted for race day. A short two blocks away, I entered the lot, parked the car, and hurried into the gym. The room was full of loud voices and the bustling movements of busy runners, checking in and picking up race shirts and numbers. I spotted Ned, the race director, who looks like a military commander. He gives orders and directs people in the same way that a general would command his troops. "Hi, Ned!" I said to him affectionately. I towered over Ned with my six-foot frame. As I hugged him, I looked over at his wife, Hannah. "Geez, Hannah, can I steal your husband away from you?" She laughed and continued helping a runner check in.

I remembered a conversation I had had with Hannah and Ned while having dinner during their recent trip to Las Vegas. Ned was telling a story about a particularly tough ultrarace he had run years back. "I was dead," he was telling me, "just dead at the end of that race."

Hannah stopped eating and looked over at me. "And," she said with a wry smile, "he's been dead ever since!" I wasn't expecting that, and I doubled over in laughter. Hannah and Ned had been married for forty years, and both had a list of accomplishments in ultrarunning.

As I checked in, Ned pulled the packet from the arms of a volunteer who was sitting behind the table. "Let me see," he said as I reached to get my packet. "What race are you running, Molly?"

"The 50K," I answered, quite sure that the 31 miles would be plenty for me to handle. I had run Rio Del Lago 100-mile race six weeks earlier and I was mentally not prepared to go further.

"Molly, run the 50-mile race," Ned persisted as I tried to take the packet out of his hands.

"Ned, I'm not up for it."

But Ned had a death grip on my packet and would not let go. We played tug of war for a few seconds. "You have all the training. Go slow and do the 50," said Ned. Mentally, I was still feeling really down from dealing with Jane, but I also felt that I couldn't say no to Ned. Emotional drama. That seemed to be my life.

With misgivings and a big sigh, I agreed. "Okay, Ned, but you're the only guy in the world who could talk me into this."

"Remember," he reminded me, "Take it slow out there. Start slow! Take a walk break about every fifteen minutes. You can do this," he said as he handed me the 50-mile packet.

Trepidations filled my mind as I pondered the next day's race. Back at the hotel room I slept that night, regretting my decision to push the distance. I dreamt that I was running all night through dense trees. When the alarm sounded at 4:00 a.m., I felt exhausted, as if I had already run the vast 50-mile distance. I dragged myself from bed, microwaved my traditional pre-race oatmeal, and began to put on my gear. Today, I knew, would be a battle. I slipped my gaiters over my running shoes to keep pebbles and dirt out of my shoes. I pulled on my running shorts with six small pockets in the back. Inside those I always carry extra tissue, Chapstick, my iPod, electrolyte tablets, and energy gels. I secured Jane's bracelet around my wrist and heard its soft jingle as I fastened the clasp. I threw on a light jacket, grabbed my keys, and stepped outside into the cold and quiet darkness. I ran to the car, trying to ward off the breeze that blew up around my neck. I switched on the lights and crept out onto the deserted streets. Within a few minutes, I pulled up to the busy parking lot where the runners were gathering in the dark. Two overhead spotlights were shining down on an arch that marked the start line.

I spotted Buddy Bill easily, since he always towers over everyone else. Bill wasn't running on this occasion. Instead, as runners often do, he was going to be supporting runners at an aid station on the course, handing out water, food, and support. He greeted me with his usual grin and hug. Then he cocked his head and stared at me. "You okay?" he asked.

"I couldn't be better," I lied. "Which aid station are you working?" I asked.

"The one that I'll see you at," he laughed, "Have a good run." Again the bear hug, which I clung to for longer than usual. Then I lined up with the runners and glanced at my watch.

"Two minutes to start," yelled Ned.

My heart skipped a beat as I mentally started to focus on the moments ahead. *You can do this, Molly*, I told myself. *Remember Jane, think of Jane.* Then a shout went out, and I started off strong, running faster than usual. I was in the front of the pack with the big boys, running for Jane. After twenty minutes, I was panting hard, and my head and heart hurt from the exertion. I continued to run aggressively, ignoring Ned's advice to start slow and walk every fifteen minutes. My thoughts were on Jane. I wanted Jane to get better. I wanted our lives to go back to normal. I didn't want to have to continue my divorce. I didn't want to have a broken family. I ran hard. I wanted to wake up Mother Earth and have her listen to me as I ran. I wanted Her to cure Jane. I believed that my intense running would spin the energy needed to cure Jane. I called out quietly, "Jane, Jane, Jane," using her name as a mantra.

Then I began experiencing an unusually sharp pain in my knee, and my pace slowed considerably. This pain was interrupting my concentration. It began to increase with every mile as I furiously tried to overcome it. After hours of slowing and stopping and trying to get control, I approached the turnaround point for the 50K race. This was the original finish line for the race that I had wanted to run. Suddenly I was overcome with regrets. I regretted that I hadn't done more to comfort my friend. I regretted that I didn't listen to Ned and start out slow. I regretted that I didn't stick with my original decision to run the 50K. Although I had slowed considerably, I stubbornly passed the 50K turnaround sign and continued another 10 miles to the 25-mile turnaround point for the 50-milers. At mile 22, I started crying. I was completely losing it.

When I approached an aid station, one of the volunteers said, "You better pick up the pace, you're pulling up the rear." That's when I realized that nearly all of the other runners had passed me. Standing in that aid station, I began to sob out loud. Someone grabbed a chair and offered it to me. I asked for some ice, put it on my knee, and acted like that injury was the cause of my tears. My knee was still screaming at me, but the tears were now from the realization that I was blowing this race. I was a disaster. How could I fail this race when it was for Jane? Maybe the pain was psychological. Was it Jane's pain haunting me? I began to sob harder, feeling sorry for myself, the lousy runner who couldn't run to save her friend.

The aid station volunteer approached me again. "Where's Bill?" he asked. "Is he running?" He was probably hoping Bill might come along and take this emotional female off his hands.

"Bill is a volunteer at another aid station," I blurted out as I wiped tears off my grimy face. "I'll be okay. Thanks for the ice." I stood up and tried not to look at his worried face. "Don't tell Bill that you saw me crying," I yelled over my shoulder as I hobbled back onto the course.

Off I continued. It was feeling more and more like I was on the death march of Bataan. I think I cried at every aid station. Everyone on the course saw the tall blonde crybaby sobbing, weaving back and forth, making her way from aid station to aid station. I should have worn a T-shirt that said, "Emotional Wreck, Stand Back, Save Yourself." I continued to unravel at every mile. All the strength and super goddess skills that I wanted to possess for Jane had collapsed. I was a female volcano overflowing with estrogen gone bad by the time I spotted Bill at mile 40. I saw him standing solemnly in the distance. That clear vision of him made new tears fall. Not only was I a disgrace to Jane, I was also a disappointment to my best friend and mentor, Buddy Bill.

"I quit!" I sobbed as he put his arms around me. "I quit. I'm miserable. I can't run. My knee hurts. And, I hate Ned!" As I made that last statement, I started to cry harder because I knew that Ned was the one person who was not to blame.

Bill calmly looked at my knee. "It's not swollen," he observed. "Is quitting what you really want?"

"No!" I yelled at him, "I'm falling apart!" I cried. "Everything sucks . . . I suck!" I ranted and raved for a few minutes as Bill calmly watched me. My mind was inconsolable. Another win for cancer, I thought bitterly.

"You haven't missed cutoff," Bill stated. "You still have ninety minutes to finish. It's up to you."

I took a big breath and closed my eyes for a moment. "I'll try to go a few more miles," I croaked. I was now one of a handful of runners left on the course, and it was getting dark. I hugged Bill and said, "Thanks for being my friend." I wiped away my tears and headed back out on the course. Now I was starting to get mad at myself. "Molly, you big wimp. You stupid dummy." I yelled out loud, "Stop your incessant whining, I can't even stand to hear you, and you're me." What a babbling mess!

With increased concentration, I began to go deep within. I needed to focus. I needed to zone out and dig deep. I went to that quiet place where I could move through space without outside interference.

At the mile-45 aid station, I saw my friend Hannah. She was waving and yelling. Bill, having just arrived from the last aid station, was walking toward us. It was obvious from Hannah's smiles that she didn't know the emotional state that I was in. Hannah was a dear friend to me. I had such respect for her accomplishments and held her in high regard as an athlete, mentor, and friend. On seeing her out there cheering me, my embarrassment and instability was ready to crack again.

"Great job, Molly!" Hannah gushed as she ran up holding a cup of water.

I slowed to a walk. I felt the dark coming on, and there was a chill in the air. I took her hand and said softly, "Hannah, I'm a mess."

Hannah stopped and examined my tear-stained face and grabbed hold of both my arms. "Honey," she said, "you just keep running . . . you just keep running, honey." Simple but effective advice. I stopped crying and glanced at Bill standing behind her observing the two of us. I forced a weak smile and thanked them. I turned and ran, heading for the cool grove of trees and a bend in the trail. I took a big breath and slowed my heart beat. I took another slow breath and concentrated on my form. I began to repeat my traditional mantra, "Run lightly. Keep moving. Relax and move. Relax and move. Move through space. Dancing. Dancing." Then, a thought passed through me. *Jane, I will finish this race even if I have to finish it on my hands and knees.* It was getting darker as I approached two people who were the last runners, besides myself, left on the course. I easily passed them with new energy infused from Hannah and Bill. I had no knee pain. For another twenty minutes I ran strong, determined to turn around my disastrous performance.

Three miles from the finish line, Bill and Hannah were again waiting for me, standing at the beginning of the levy, two steadfast figures monitoring my progress. "You are doing just fine, honey," Hannah said as I ran past. "You are almost home." The look of concern on both their faces made me sad.

I turned another corner as I heard Bill talking to Hannah in hushed tones. "If she makes it to the finish line before cutoff, it will be an incredible comeback."

I needed a comeback. I hadn't expected to finish the race in the dark. I looked at my watch under a park lamp and realized that I had thirty minutes to finish the last three miles. Ten-minute miles. I can do that! I had been on the course for eleven hours and thirty minutes. Almost all of that time was consumed by a meltdown of epic proportions. Official cutoff was twelve hours. After that I'd be labeled DNF (did not finish). I couldn't bear the thought of being labeled DNF on top of all my other traumatic failures.

When I reached the far end of the levy, I was suddenly overcome with confusion. It was now pitch black and my little headlamp seemed tiny in the dark. I couldn't remember which way to go. The hours of emotional torment had taken a toll. I looked at my watch and hit the light. The green glow showed that I had to make the finish line in fifteen minutes. Panic set in. I ran to the left, into the jet black depths, but the only sound was my ragged breathing as I tore through the underbrush onto a fork in the road. A fork in the road? I didn't remember that. Where were the course ribbons and markings? This wasn't right. I heard a rustling of leaves to my right. Not a wild animal . . . dear God! Black darkness was all around. I shined my headlamp to illuminate the brush more clearly. Nothing. Five minutes until the end of the race!

"BILL, BILL!" I became hysterical, "BILL, I'M LOST!" New tears began to spill. I looked again at my watch as the time escaped. I ran up and down the trail realizing that nothing looked familiar. Where were the runners I had passed just a short while ago? Why hadn't they passed me? I tore off my headlamp and glared at my watch. The race had just ended. The rustling in the leaves began again. Furious with myself, I glared in the direction of that mysterious noise and shouted, "I DON'T GIVE A SHIT IF YOU ARE A COUGAR IN THERE. I'M READY TO TAKE YOU ON!" The leaves became quiet.

I collapsed onto the dirt path, shaking and choking with angry sobs. The wind was blowing and I was cold. *No one is going to find you here, Molly.* I picked myself up and again retraced my steps back toward the levy. As I reached the top, I tried to hear the sounds of people. I knew the finish line had to be near. I looked out over the top of the levy into the vast distance where I could see the small town of Auburn. The wind blew my hair back from my face as I watched the blinking lights miles away. I thought my heart would break. "I am so sorry, Jane," I whispered. I sat and waited for someone to find me. All my energy was spent.

"MOLLY!" shouted a familiar masculine voice.

"I'm here, Bill, I'm over here!" I started running in the direction of his voice. I saw his silhouette in the shadows and ran full onto his chest, burying my head into his shoulder as I wrapped my arms tight around him, clinging as if to a life preserver in the middle of the ocean. "I am so sorry, Buddy. I'm so very sorry. I blew it. I blew the whole race."

"What happened?" he asked as he stroked my hair. "Tell me what happened."

I was blinded by tears as I sobbed out my tale of woe, the dismal end of a dreadful day. I don't remember my words. I just blubbered out the last of the frustration and anguish. Bill kept his arms wrapped around me half lifting me off the path, as he listened to my descriptions of losing my way. "You made the turn too soon," he said, "You went about three miles off course." I looked up and realized that if I had continued straight, I would have found my way back to the finish line and a thousand lights. As we trudged along, I took in huge gulps of air in an attempt to force my body to relax.

Bill calmed me, "It's okay, Molly. You are now a certified ultra-runner. There isn't any one of us who hasn't gotten lost. You are in good company." He tugged at my hair in a playful way. "Listen," he said softly as the gravel crunched under our feet, "Ned is really worried about you. He'll feel awful if he sees you cry. When you see him, just tell him that you loved the race so much that you wanted to stay out on the course longer than anyone else." He grinned and hugged me close.

"Okay, Bill. And by the way, thank you for being my friend." We stopped and hugged, surrounded by the blowing wind.

"Come on," he said. "Time to go." We walked in silence for a few more minutes, then rounded the corner to the finish line. The door to the hall was open, shedding light out into the darkness. A volunteer was rolling up the finish line sign, and another person was unhooking the lights to close up shop. A small group of people was loading the last of the supplies into boxes. I realized how late I really was.

Ned spotted me and rushed over. "Are you okay? What happened?" I could tell he was masking real concern.

"First of all, I loved your race, Ned. I just couldn't bear to stop." He was scrutinizing my tear-stained, dirty face as I spoke. "Seriously, Ned," I continued, "I am so sorry to worry you. I made a wrong turn and screwed up. I really am perfectly fine." I gave him a big hug.

"Next year, Ned, I'm coming back to this race to redeem myself. It really is a beautiful course."

Hannah came over and hugged me, too. "I have gotten lost in my share of races," she stated. "There isn't a good runner among us that hasn't had that experience." I was thankful for her words.

Then I realized I was starving! All the food was packed up. "Bill" I pleaded.

"Yeah, let's go eat," he said. I grabbed my bag and we started for the door.

"Wait," Ned yelled. He brought over a race certificate that said *50 Mile Finisher.* "Take this home, Molly." He said as he handed it to me. "You completed the distance. Well done."

"Wait," he said, then pulled out a frame from a box at the table and placed the certificate inside. "There you go," he smiled.

"Thanks, Ned," I said. At that moment I felt so much love for my friends. "Good night, everyone. Thank you," I called to the remaining people, and we walked to the car.

Funny thing about that race. I worked out a lot of my sadness back there. I worked out a lot of life's heavy burdens. I left them on a trail in the wilderness. I left them on the path to be blown by the wind and covered by the leaves.

I swung my exhausted legs into the car. *Oh Jane. One day when you are cured of cancer and we are old women sitting in our rocking chairs, we will laugh about the day that your dorky friend got lost in a 50-mile race to cure your cancer. And we will sip our tea and remember that we both shared a lot of adventures on our road of friendship.* I laid my head back on the seat and felt grateful for my life . . . and thankful for my friends. As of this writing, January 2014, Jane is cancer free. Thank God.

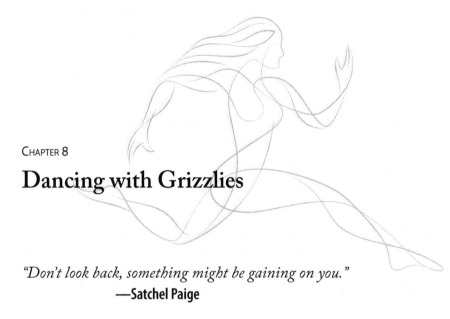

CHAPTER 8

Dancing with Grizzlies

"Don't look back, something might be gaining on you."
—Satchel Paige

IS THERE ANYTHING scarier than the idea of being eaten alive by an enormous angry grizzly bear? Anyone who has ever entered a primeval forest has to weigh the risks. What should I do upon encountering some huge and hairy beast lurking within the trees? These thoughts were haunting me as the plane touched down in Kalispell, in the northwest corner of Montana across from Canada, just as a snowstorm moved in.

The same old thoughts kept popping into my head: *Whose idea was this? Oh Molly, you are in over your head again!* On our drive to Glacier National Park, I read the Forest Service brochure, especially the large letters that read: "WARNING! People have died due to grizzly bear attacks." I had signed up for the 50-mile "Le Grizz" run while I was roasting in 110-degree July weather in Las Vegas. At that time the October race sounded like an exotic wonderland of cool air, snowcapped mountains, and beautiful streams. I had visions of pristine lakes, crystal hanging icicles, big sky, and meadows of ancient pines. Those intoxicating images blinded me to the reality of a freezing wilderness with shin-deep snow under desolate grey skies and especially . . . grizzly bears.

I suppose every child battles a particular deep-seated fear. I had girlfriends who were scared of snakes, sharks, imaginary boogeymen and monsters. The most terrifying image that I had long-ago banished from my brain was the thought of being shredded by the six-inch pointed claws of a massive grizzly bear.

When I first read THE WARNING in the comfort and safety of my home in Las Vegas, my diaphragm seized up when I read. I was about to leave the safety of my little kitchen and travel to the bears . . . as if I were looking for them. I read that warning a dozen times. But it all seemed like pretend until that plane touched down on Montana soil.

I was thankful my dear friend Pam Everett had decided to crew me on this unusual adventure. Pam is a warm weather runner like me. Our spur of the moment Montana adventure was concocted because Pam had business in Montana. We were completely unprepared for the weather. (Apparently they don't know about Indian summers in northwest Montana.) Our brief exposure to the Montana air while traveling from the airport to our motel convinced us that our Las Vegas clothes were not going to cut it.

After spending a small fortune on tights, long underwear, mittens, hand and feet warmers, scarves, and a beanie, I climbed into my cozy hotel room bed and dreamed of running swiftly through the forest. It won't be that bad, I reasoned to myself as I tossed and turned. They can't have a race where the bears are mauling people on the race course, for God's sake! The 3:00 a.m. alarm shocked us awake. Pam and I jumped up and got ourselves ready for the two and a half hour drive. Running out to the car, screaming and laughing hysterically at our insane circumstance, we felt the biting cold through four layers of clothing. But then we both grew quiet on the drive. It was a surreal feeling driving through the empty town of Hungry Horse in the pitch black. We stopped the car once just to stand outside and look at millions of stars twinkling in the night sky. It was almost a full moon so there was a shimmer on the snow-covered trees in the forest.

We arrived at the starting line where cars were parked along the snow-lined trail road. Bundled-up runners were stomping around slapping their hands on their arms trying to stay warm. We stared wide-eyed when mounds of snow beside the road began moving and shifting. Men began to emerge. They had spent the night in tents that were covered in snow. The race start point was in such a remote locale that runners, tough Jeremiah Johnson types, had slept overnight at the start line. They were a wild-looking bunch with disheveled hair and beards. We were in the midst of Neanderthal ultrarunners, which made me feel even more out of place in my pink parka with braids poking out the bottom of my white beanie. Nervous energy led me to mask my fear and anxiety by spouting, "Good morning, everyone!" I got some curious stares.

One guy asked if I was going to be manning an aid station. When I told him I was a runner, he looked incredulous and asked, "You are running THIS race? Where are you from?"

"Vegas, Baby!" I smiled with my arms outstretched. He shook his head and walked away. These men were from Canada, Nova Scotia, and Alaska. I couldn't have felt more out of place. I tried not to think about the cold as I bounced around waiting for the start. The wind began blowing as dawn was creeping in. I was excited to be pushing myself beyond the limits of my normal endurance in a setting of extreme wilderness. On the other hand, I was surrounded by people who were obviously questioning my ability and my sanity. Although I was accustomed to curious looks, I wondered about my ability to run at those temps in such a strange and foreboding environment.

Pat Cafferty, the rough and rugged race director, grabbed his shotgun and headed toward the start line. Pam and I were jumping up and down hugging each other with anticipation. "Have a great run!" said Pam. "I'll drive the car a couple miles ahead and check to see how you're doing. Then I'll pace you later on." I lined up with the beards and camouflaged parkas while Pat gave his final instructions.

"Okay, everyone, listen up," he said. "There are grizzlies and black bears in this region. If you see a bear, climb a tree. Now good luck!" Then, without warning, he blasted his shotgun into the night sky. The thunderous explosion ignited my nervous energy, which shot me up straight into the air. Before I could regain my composure, I noticed that the Neanderthals had started running. Like a tall, thin pink flamingo in a heard of rhinos, I began running with the pack.

Although every joint ached from the cold, I felt secure in the midst of those tough men. Even if they couldn't save me from a grizzly bear, I'd be relatively safe if I could remain in the middle of the pack. But everyone else was running so fast. My body with its thin Las Vegas blood seemed to have solidified from the cold. I could barely force one foot in front of the other. One by one, the other runners disappeared into the distance. Where are the security guards to keep the bears away?

A tall lanky man ran up beside me and we chatted for a few minutes. His name was Skookumtumtum, a Black Foot Indian, who had been running this race for the last twenty-five years. He told me I was in for a treat because the course ran alongside some of the most beautiful country on the planet. I wanted to ask him just one simple question. "Hey, Skook, in the twenty-five years of running this race, have you seen any grizzlies on the course?" But I first asked myself, *Molly, do you REALLY want that answer? Do you really, under these circumstances, at this particular time, running on the course in the middle of the Montana wilderness, do you WANT that answer?* No. I wanted ignorance and peace. So I ran.

I was soon at the back of the pack with another runner who had two bells attached to his waist. Ah ha! I'll run with the guy with bells. What a brilliant idea. Bells scare bears!! Ding ding. Ding ding. Ding ding. The guy didn't talk. In fact, there was no other sound. Ding ding. Ding ding. Ding ding. Within twenty minutes those damn bells were driving me nuts. They were incessant. I couldn't stand them any longer as I slowed my pace and listened to him disappear ahead. I would have to face the bears alone.

Bears, bears, bears. I couldn't think of anything else. I pictured a huge brown monster jumping from the trees and clawing my intestines out as I screamed in agony. STOP!!!! Positive thoughts!! Positive! I calmed down. I thought about Wayne Dyer and Tony Robbins. Think Positive! So I began reassembling my thoughts, but since my subconscious mind had been focused exclusively on bears, I had to alter my thoughts gradually. Yogi Bear . . . Booboo . . . Happy Dancing Bears . . . that's it, that's it. Meanwhile, I scanned the trail ahead as I continued to run, far away from Bell Man and Skook. I could climb that tree, and from there, that tree, and from there, I could climb that one. My mind began to calm. Hey, I can do this thing!

I spotted Pam up ahead next to our car parked on the side of the snow-dusted road. She was jumping up and down trying to stay warm as she waited for me to reach her. "We did not bring any food," she reported as I approached. "I hope the aid stations along the course have food for you."

"I don't care about food," I replied. "Just go ahead and make lots of noise to keep the bears away from me!" Pam laughed, jumped into the warm car, and sped away.

Around the next curve in the road, I saw the first aid station. A man who looked like one of the ZZ Top band members was sitting in a chair next to the aid station. There was a frozen pitcher of water and a half empty bag of frozen potato chips. "Howdy," he drawled.

"How far to the next aid station?" I asked.

"No idea," he said. "I just came out to watch you all." That was helpful.

As I ran through the day, I was surprised that my body never warmed up despite the exertion. I couldn't feel my face. My breath caused great puffs of frosty air. My stomach hurt from the constant stress. I focused my attention on the beautiful trees and tried to remember how to say a Hail Mary. As the afternoon sun was setting, I began to face the reality that I would have to finish the race in the dark. The end of Le Grizz is legendary. For the last 400 meters, the trail ends. There is nothing but bushes and dense forest, apparently part of an ancient Black Foot Indian initiation tradition.

Pam was standing beside the car alongside the road near the bush-whacking area. I made Pam position the car and aim the headlights into the dark forest where I would have to run. Even though the car lights did not penetrate far into the foliage, that beam of light was sufficient to propel me forward. I don't remember ever being so scared in my life. It reminded me of my brother locking me in a dark closet, which used to freak me out. Only this time the dark closet might contain a bear waiting for me.

I ran into the grove of trees wishing I was a real Black Foot Indian with a tomahawk for protection. I crashed through the underbrush. Up the hill I ran, pulling myself up by holding onto trees, climbing, kicking, fighting my way through the foliage. Branches pulled at my clothes, making me feel as if I were under assault. Although exhausted, the ensuing panic propelled me faster. I thought I heard someone scream in fear only to realize it was me. When it seemed as if the nightmare would never end, I suddenly burst into a clearing, my hair full of leaves and dirt. There was a bright campfire with runners gathered round. The finish line!

Everyone around the bonfire seemed happy and relaxed as they glanced over at the tall but disheveled pink flamingo who had just popped out of the bush-whacking area. I patted down my hair and strolled into their area, pretending that the last twelve hours was a piece of cake.

Yep . . . it's just me, I thought to myself as I calmly walked into the circle of runners. Just call me by my Indian name: "Not Killed by Grizzlies." I sat next to the campfire, and the tension in my mind and body slowly dissipated. Pam was even happier than me, glad that her never-ending crew job was finished. We ate corn on the cob and chicken as we celebrated surviving the Montana wilderness.

Nope . . . I'll never be doing that race again!

Molly in the Sahara Desert—Marathon Des Sables

CHAPTER 9

Marathon Des Sables—Africa

"It's a dangerous business Bilbo, walking out one's front door."

—Gandalf in J.R.R. Tolkien, *The Hobbit*

THE SAND WHIPPED and whirled stinging my face. Trying desperately to get relief from the brutal gale force winds, I closed my eyes and pulled my neck buff up to cover my face. My shoulders and back ached. I grabbed the shoulder straps of my backpack while I yanked and shifted my body, trying to relieve some of the pressure points.

Visibility was next to nil. I did not have a clue where I was or how far I was from the next human being. I braced myself against the wind and tried to problem-solve. I could rest and wait out the storm, but there was no shelter, and I was exerting energy attempting to stand upright. I could sit and cover my head, but the thought of being buried by the sand made me shudder. Could I retrace my steps? I glanced behind me where I'd walked moments before, but my tracks had already disappeared.

When I had checked in for the Marathon Des Sables 150-mile race in Morocco, race officials insisted that we carry a compass in our backpack. Race officials apparently assumed that a group of international ultra marathon runners were adept at such rudimentary navigational devices. Their assumption was undoubtedly correct . . . except for Molly Sheridan, mother of three.

The true function of a compass had always eluded me. That little arrow was always quivering and pointing in some direction that was different than where I wanted to go. What good is that? There had been times when my brother Ted had attempted to explain how a compass works, but his words sounded suspiciously like those of my high school geometry teacher. On both occasions, upon hearing words like "degrees" and "angles," my mind took up a pleasant tune and telepathically transported itself into a garden with blooming flowers and colorful butterflies. Had it ever occurred to me that I might one day be lost, all by myself in a killer sandstorm in the middle of the Sahara Desert, I probably would have at least tried to pay attention. Now I might die because of that superficial attitude.

I wanted to kick myself, but I was too exhausted to do anything but continue to stand upright, leaning into the buffeting winds. I was incredulous that I was in the middle of the Sahara Desert in North Africa trying to conquer one of the fiercest, toughest footraces on the planet. It was kind of funny really. Here I was lost in the middle of nowhere with winds blowing me this way and that, not knowing which direction to take next. This was exactly where I was in my personal life—uncharted territory, pushed this way and that by forces beyond my control, not sure which direction I should take.

I stood atop that sand dune leaning against the wind and thought back to what had brought me here. It was one small little decision, a whim really, that brought me halfway around the world. When deciding whether to go, I was ticking off two lists in my head: the risks of going and the reasons for staying at home. I remembered the risk list had been much longer than the staying list. But at that moment, standing on the sand dune facing fear, possibly even death,

I could not remember what convinced me to go in spite of the known risks and hardships.

I remembered reading about the Frenchman who got lost during this Marathon Des Sables race a few years back. A giant wind storm turned him around on the course, and he was lost for nine days. The race officials found him alive but dehydrated and blathering about making poor decisions and lists he had made. I thought about the race regulations which read, "In case of a Sahara Desert wind storm, stop, cover yourself with your safety blanket, and wait for the wind to pass. If you are in danger, send up your flare." I hadn't figured out how to use the flare, either. It was big and bulky and reminded me of a giant firecracker, which scared me. I knew I wasn't going to need that! Seven hundred runners in the desert. How can you possibly get lost? Everyone around me would have a flare.

I stood there for a long time . . . on that mound . . . with the roar of the wind and swirling sand my only reality. There was no another human being in sight. Maybe no one was within miles of me. The realization that I am a mortal human being began to haunt me. Mother Nature rules in the Sahara Desert. No doubt I had pushed myself too quickly. I had gone from innocent beginner jogging around my neighborhood to scary North Africa, lost, pondering my fate on a 150-mile stage race that Newsweek labeled the toughest foot race on the planet.

I was getting pissed off at myself. Why was I so directionally challenged? I thought about the last race I had gotten lost in. Well, actually, I'd been lost more than once. Sometimes I zoned out and didn't pay attention to course markings. It wasn't unusual for me to miss the orange flagging and run straight ahead when I was supposed to turn. But this was different; there were no course markings in the Sahara Desert. My stomach knotted with the fear and anxiety.

I had decided to go to North Africa, the exotic Marathon Des

Sable, six-day stage race through the Sahara Desert, as I was sitting comfortably in my jammies at home surfing the Internet. I stumbled onto the race by accident and registered on a whim. A few months later, I found myself alone on a flight to Morocco. I had volunteered to raise funds for the kids at Boys Town Nevada, and I thought the adventure might benefit the kids and their organization.

After notifying my family, brother Sean had sent his "words of encouragement." He began by telling me that he thought I was an idiot. Then he reminded me that I was un-athletic and jumped to the conclusion that I was trying to kill myself. I had saved his email so I could prove him wrong, but now the word idiot seemed to be an apt description.

The boyish face of Dr. Mean appeared before me as a ghostly apparition. "You are too old," he proclaimed. I did not want to see him proven right.

I thought back to the events and challenges within my life since my first marathon in Washington, D.C. three years before. The shift in my life and the internal call to adventure brought out my stubbornness, my inner rebel. I wasn't twenty years old, but damn, don't mess with me! Thinking back on the whole doc episode stiffened my resolve and made me mad once again.

I compared my present predicament in dry, blowing sand to almost drowning a couple of days before. When we arrived in Morocco, there were huge rains that flooded our town and some of our camps. They called it the 100-year flood in the Sahara. The bus that transported us to our first camp attempted to cross a rushing river much to the dismay of all the foreigners aboard. In fact, we were all yelling at the bus driver not to cross the rushing river.

I remembered my brother Brian warning me before I left home for the trip: "Remember," Brian said, "don't get your biddy in a wadi." When I asked him what in the world he was talking about, he repeated, "Don't get your biddy in a wadi." He then explained that I should never put my bivouac (biddy or campsite) in a wash (wadi) because I would get flooded and washed away. I told him that I didn't think I need to worry about flooding in the Sahara.

The bus full of runners entered the rushing waters. I looked at the surprised expressions on the faces of others sitting around me. We were stunned that the bus driver was attempting to forge the river. The bus was momentarily lifted and began floating sideways. Panicked passengers began yelling and trying to pry off the small hammers on the interior of the bus wall to break the glass and jump out. At the last minute the bus wheels grabbed the dirt and rocks churning beneath us, and we were able to make it to the other side. But it was a traumatic ride. Everyone was completely freaked out, including me. We arrived at our destination only to find that our camp had been swept away. We moved into a small town called Erdu and stayed at a humble hotel until the race officials could transport us to another location.

I brushed off the sand that was stuck to my body and adjusted my goggles. My best guess was to go straight. I began to lean into the wind and plod through the shifting sand. I had never felt so alone.

Some indeterminable time later, I discerned images moving in the distance. Then they disappeared. A mirage? Wait! There they were again. They were real. Three ghostly figures, wavering images, kept appearing and disappearing in the haze. I squinted and moved towards them wondering if they were runners, nomads, or figures of my imagination. "Hey, over here!" I called, waving my arms. They couldn't hear me.

Soon I could see their backpacks with water bottles attached to their shoulder straps. Other runners! Men who knew which way to go! I felt like I had been rescued although no one other than me knew that I was lost. I yelled again, "Guys! Do you know where we are? Do you know what direction we're supposed to be going?"

All three glanced up with startled looks. I hadn't stopped to realize that I might appear every bit as much as a ghost as they appeared to me. In unison, they asked, "Where did you come from?"

I didn't recognize them. I knew there were only fifty Americans at Marathon De Sables that year. I had met many of them when I arrived in Casablanca to switch planes to Ouarzazate, and others when we congregated in long lines at check-in, which took hours. All our required supplies had to be confirmed before we were allowed to enter the race. Anyone who didn't have the proper food and equipment would not be allowed to run. I used the time to chat with the international runners. Everyone got to know each other. But I couldn't place these guys. Of course, their hats, goggles, and scarves didn't help. I raised my voice to be heard above the howling wind. "Are you guys Americans?"

The big heavyset runner replied, "Canadian."

That's why I didn't recognize them. The Canadians had been in a different group at camp. Each nationality was set up in groups of tents: Americans, Canadians, Australians, etc. The largest group consisted of 700 smoking Frenchman. Smoking ultramarathoners was something I hadn't seen before. Of course, the Marathon Des Sables is a race organized by the French. Race regulations required that each runner be completely self-supported; everything had to be carried in a backpack to survive a week in the Sahara Desert. At checkpoints during the race we received rations of bottled water, two to four liters depending upon the distance. That ration of water was primarily for drinking, but I also used it sparingly to wash, brush my teeth, make a small cup of coffee with my miniature stove, or boil water for my freeze-dried camp food. Water was a precious commodity so washing my long hair was out. The neck buff was used not only to cover my hair, which was grimier by the day, but also to cover my face when the sand was blowing.

I had never run a stage race before. Every day began with a map and coordinates laying out the kilometers required to run to reach the next bivouac. I spent a lot of time converting kilometers into miles. The day-to-day distance varied. One day 18 miles was required to be completed, the next day 26 miles. The longest distance was 50 miles, but runners were allotted extra time to get to camp for that long day. If a runner failed to reach the next camp in the allotted time, he (or she) would be pulled from the race and sent home. The fact that this was an unacceptable outcome motivated me to keep running.

I repeated, "Do you know where you're going?" That sounded kind of stupid after the words left my mouth.

The tall man nearest to me leaned close and pointed to a black packet strapped to his arm. "I have a solar GPS system."

The other two runners pulled up close to him to scan their maps. They looked like they knew what they were doing. That sounded better than a compass or a flare. Modern technology in the Sahara Desert! For the next few hours, those three men became my dearest friends. They were never out of my sight . . . or even out of reach.

I never did find out their names. There was never a moment to stop for introductions or social graces. All I knew was that I was so relieved and happy to have humans around me. I had a second chance, and I promised myself that if I came back to this godforsaken territory, I was going to learn to read a compass. Or maybe a solar GPS. I didn't know what that was, but if I was ever in the middle of the Sahara Desert again, lost in a sandstorm, I sure wanted one.

The Canadians were fast, hard-core runners. I was terrified that they were going to disappear and leave me alone again. As we raced along the sands, I wondered if there was a similar but less-terrifying way to motivate myself in upcoming races. Down the sand dunes we ran, then back up a giant mountain of sand, then down again into blowing misery. I kept pace although my muscles were screaming in pain. We ran through horrible conditions for hours. I had no idea how far it was to the checkpoint. My legs ached from the stinging sand and straining muscles; my feet were raw from sand seeping into my shoes despite my gaiters around my ankles. I had ordered these particular gaiters from England because they were designed to protect my feet from "grime, rocks, and dirt." The sands of the Sahara, however, are so fine that it is impossible to keep them out of your shoe. The sand was inevitable and so were the resulting blisters. I knew I had humongous blisters. I stopped periodically to dump sand from my shoes, but more blew in before I could get my shoe back on. No matter what I did, there was no escaping the sand and no escaping the intense pain from the blisters. Witnessing the condition of other feet throughout the race, gigantic blisters were apparently one of the hardships runners were expected to endure.

After endless hours of unending pain and discomfort, I could see, off in the distance, the campsite. And that marked the conclusion of . . . day one. I had six more days of fear and agony ahead of me. I had run only 18 miles, but my body felt like it had been 80. My pack was so heavy, my feet macerated, my muscles ached. I wondered how in the world I would get through six more days of this.

After picking up my ration of four liters of water, I made my way through the line of tents. The Berber tribe never seemed to pick any campsite with soft ground even though we were surrounded by sand dunes. After being alone all day out in the desert, I arrived at a tent with seven other runners piled in. Floor space was minimal. I stepped over runners who were stretched out on the ground like they had just finished a battle. My emotions were raw—a cross between crying and wanting to scream or punch someone. A young Australian woman named Ineke was brewing tea. She looked in great shape after her first day. We waved to each other, but we were too tired to chat. I saw that Terry from Michigan was rolled up in his sleeping bag sound asleep. If you were faster, I thought to myself, you could be asleep and comfortable in a sleeping bag at this very moment.

I passed George Velasco, whom I had met at the hotel where all the Americans stayed the night before we headed into the Sahara Desert. Everyone knew him and he was well liked; however, he rubbed me the wrong way with his dumb jokes. Noticing that George was awake in his comfortable sleeping bag, I blurted, "George, you really pissed me off at race check-in." George appeared shocked, but I wasn't finished. "I didn't appreciate your dumb-blonde joke aimed at me. I thought it was insulting. Just to let you know." The pain and discomfort caused by desert running does weird things to people. For me, it brought out a brand of aggression that rarely ever surfaced in my normal life. I was tired and miserable, and George was my nearest target.

"Hey, I'm really sorry." He got up (no easy effort) and walked toward me. His face was streaked with dirt and his hair was wind-blown and disheveled. He had two round burn holes in the front part of his T-shirt like a giant snake had bitten him. "Sometimes I say really stupid stuff. I am sincerely sorry." He tilted his head down and looked at the ground.

Now I felt bad. The poor guy. He was as tired and uncomfortable as me, but some bitchy woman he barely knew had just lashed out, made him feel bad and, worst of all, made him get out of bed. Because I was super cranky, I was taking it out on this poor guy. I looked down at the holes on his shirt and tried to change the subject. "What happened to your shirt? Those look like burn holes."

"I came upon a runner passed out on the course." He rubbed his hand through his hair, exhausted. "I had to send off a flare to get medical attention. When I snapped the flare, it misfired and hit me in the stomach." He lifted his shirt to show me the red, angry burns all over his torso.

Now I felt even worse. Here I was belittling a guy who had hero-ically saved another runner just hours before. "Oh George, I am so sorry. Do you need some help?"

"No, I'm okay. I need to go over to the medical tent to have these burns treated, and I need to check on the runner who passed out. Race management is sending him home. He was severely dehydrated."

I didn't know what to say. The runner he saved could have been me, and now, instead of sleeping, he was following up to ensure that the other guy was okay.

He gave me a mournful look. "Sorry again about the jokes. I thought maybe you would think they were funny. No offense intended. I hope we can still be friends."

I gave George a big hug and assured him that all was forgiven. "I'm so sorry I talked like that. I'm just so tired and miserable. I took it out on you. Please forgive me."

"No problem," George assured me as he walked out of the tent.

Feeling like the world's biggest jerk, I threw down my pack. On the positive side, I was thankful that I was sheltered from the unre-lenting wind, even though my "home" was only a lean-to with just three sides. I unrolled my flimsy foam mattress that I used against the stone hard ground, collapsed, and pulled my sleeping bag around my shoulders. I was grimy, filthy, and dirty. Grains of sand were on every inch and in every crevice of my body. My eyes hurt to blink. Smelling the aroma of other people's cooking—Lipton onion soup mix, hot tea, saffron rice, and some sort of beef stew—I realized I was starving. I pulled my miniature stove out of my backpack and struggled to boil some water even though my hands were shaking from fatigue. I thought about the twenty-five pounds of crap in that bag. The more I ate, the less my pack would weigh tomorrow. Maybe that would make me happier and less likely to attack some innocent guy who was gallantly saving people. George would probably come across me tomorrow, lying in the desert and dying of dehydration. I could picture him stepping over my body and leaving me for dead. What a pain in the ass, he would say to himself. What a dumb blonde!

Desperate to join other sleeping runners, I pulled out my little REI dried food packs. Hmmm, beef stroganoff or chicken with rice? They both looked exactly alike and, based on prior experience, tasted the same. After wolfing down the food, I took a look at my blistered feet. Although they were in need of some first aid, I had only enough energy to wash off the sand. I hunkered down in my sleeping bag, zipped myself in, and tried ignore the rocks stabbing my back. I slept like the dead.

The next morning I awoke to a commotion and opened my eyes to find a huge Berber tribesman in a blue turban taking down the tent. We were not scheduled to start running for three hours. Nevertheless, the tribesman collapsed the tent, leaving me and the other prostrate runners in the blowing wind and sand. I was at least thankful that the wind was not as strong as it had been the day before. Other tents were still up. Later, I learned that they always took down the Americans' tents first. When I asked about this, I found out that the race officials catered to the Frenchmen, whose tents always came down last, giving them more time to sleep within a protected shelter. Americans were the low men on the totem pole.

I pulled out my map and read the instructions for the second day's stage run. Struggling to control the rustling pages, I tried to get a sense of direction. We had twenty-two miles to cover that day over the largest sand dunes in the world—the Erg Chebi, which I was excited to see. I administered ointment to my blisters and attempted to bandage them as best I could. Then I gathered my belongings and stuffed them into my backpack, which I was beginning to regard as some sort of sinister burden.

I had a great day . . . relatively speaking. We ran through small little oases and salt flats in between the dunes. I slowed in a little village and gave the kids some candy. Their mothers with veiled faces were watched closely. That night at camp, however, I didn't feel well. I tried to get down some soup but nothing seemed appetizing.

The next to last day was the big 50-miler. I had been looking forward to the challenge, but during the night my stomach started feeling queasy, and I had terrible cramps. Then I started vomiting. Food and water were passing through me at lightning speed. So I would not disturb my tent mates, I spent most of the night away from my bivouac wrenching in the desert. At 2:00 a.m. I found the medics' tent and asked for help. No one spoke anything but French. I tried to point to my stomach and my head. In response, the French doctor gave me some pills, but they had no effect.

Dawn came and the tents were taken down. I tried to stand up but my legs were so weak I could barely support myself. The race was about to begin and I hadn't been able to hold anything down for over twelve hours. My choice was to either to start running or pull out of the race. I headed out for the course. That day was one of the worst of my life. I consulted Lynne Hewett, one of the runners in our group who was also a nurse, and she remarked that I probably had dysentery. She told me to keep sipping ginger tea and soup. Even if I kept throwing up, I should keep sipping because something would get down to my stomach.

So I sipped and struggled out in the Sahara all day and into the night for 50 tough miles over a rocky jagged mountain. I dragged myself all day in the heat, with both ends of my body emptying itself.

That night I made it to an aid station. The French nurse told me I was severely dehydrated and made me lie in a tent to recover. She gave me awful tasting salt water and told me I couldn't leave until I drank the whole thing. I didn't want to be pulled from the race so I started sipping. It made me puke. When she wasn't looking I poured most of it out the side of the tent. A Canadian with a condition similar to mine came in and lay down next to me. He introduced himself as Ian and said he was quitting. He looked over at me and asked if I was dropping out as well. I told him I refused to quit and be sent home. As soon as the sun came up, I was going to head back out on the course and he should join me. (I was attempting to talk myself into continuing as much as him.) He said he admired my gumption, but he didn't think he could make it.

In the morning, dizzy and weak, I crawled out of the tent and stood. I looked back in at Ian and said, "You might as well come with me. Otherwise, you are going to sit here all day." He crawled out and I could see the doubt in his eyes. "Look, I'm not trying to talk you into this, but they will not be able to get you to the finish with everyone else for hours. You might as well make it on your own."

So he walked with me. We were like two zombies dragging through the desert. After hours and hours through the torturous heat, weak and sick, we approached the finish line of the race. All my tent mates were waiting for me, knowing that I had been so sick for two days. The first one to welcome me was George. He gave me a huge hug and said he was proud of me. I was so grateful to see him. Then I saw Steve, Becky, Jane, Tess, Ineke, Terry, Colleen, Jay, Hans, the whole group. Everyone had made it.

Ian came up and hugged me fiercely. "I would never have made it without you." He started sobbing, "I am forever grateful."

When the race was over, the organizers flew the French Opera and Symphony out to the desert. That last night in camp, under a star-studded sky, an international group of dirty and filthy runners listened to beautiful symphonic classics. The experience brought tears to my eyes. Another glorious adventure.

CHAPTER 10

The White Line of Badwater—135 miles

"It's time to suck it up."

—Bailey Sheridan, 18 year old crew chief, giving instruction to crew in 126 degree heat at Badwater Ultramarathon"

MY BODY WAS under assault by extreme nauseating heat from all sides. I felt like I was running in hot coals inside an oven broiler. The word "hot" seemed totally inadequate to describe my condition. I was beyond hot. I was in hell.

I thought about Father O'Conner's sermon about hell that had gripped my ten-year-old heart with fear: "If you should die with a mortal sin on your soul, you will descend straight into the burning fires of hell. The pain will be excruciating—beyond description. At least in hell, I thought to myself, I wouldn't have to keep running and running and running.

Rumor has it that it was 124 degrees in Death Valley on race day, July 13th, 2009. I was running the race of my life, the Badwater Ultramarathon. It was renowned as the biggest, baddest, 135-mile non-stop race on the planet. Starting 200 feet below sea level, our destination was Mt. Whitney. It seemed like 200 degrees radiating off the payment. It was like nothing I had ever experienced.

When I returned from Marathon Des Sables eight weeks earlier, I was weak from dysentery. My body was shattered. I picked up the phone and called Lisa Smith-Batchen, a nine-time Badwater finisher. I knew she could help me prepare for the race. She had incredible experience and talent as an athlete and had firsthand knowledge of what it was like running Badwater. She laid out a plan for me that I followed to the letter. I was fortunate to live close enough that I could train directly in Death Valley.

I had applied to run the Badwater Ultramarathon race in 2008. Applicants need to have proven race records and every application goes before a committee, which decides if the runner will be accepted to the race. Only ninety runners from around the world are chosen each year from hundreds of applicants. I was rejected in 2008 for not having enough experience. This didn't sit well with me. I was reminded of the doctor who told me I was too old.

After that rejection, I decided to run seventeen races, including thirteen ultra marathons in one year. I was also accepted to run the Marathon Des Sable race in Africa. As I was getting ready to leave for Morocco, I received a letter from Race Director Chris Kostman informing me that I had been accepted into the 2009 Badwater. That was great news. The bad news was that I had already made arrangements to go to North Africa and the Sahara Desert. I would be running the two toughest footraces on the planet with barely an eight-week break in between.

Weight loss has been a problem for me. I can easily lose five to ten pounds over the course of 100 miles in thirty hours when I had little excess to begin with. With the added dysentery complication in Morocco, I had lost fifteen pounds. When I climbed off the plane from the Sahara Desert to Las Vegas, Bailey and Taylor were shocked. Taylor looked me over and kiddingly said, "I only have half a mommy!"

Therefore, I was facing the seemingly contradictory goals of training hard in the Death Valley heat, while at the same time gaining back the fifteen pounds. I didn't dare slack off the training, so I

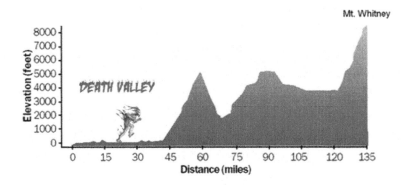

Badwater Elevation Profile

simply ate protein shakes and carbs whenever I had the chance.

I trained hard preparing myself for the barrage of heat that I was going to encounter at Badwater. Temperatures in July range from 115–125 degrees. I sauna-trained every day for the weeks leading up to the race. Living in Las Vegas was an advantage of sorts as I drove around town with no air conditioning in my car. I tried turning off the air at home to further condition myself, but my daughters threatened rebellion, and I refrained from further parental abuse. Still, when race day came, it was a shocker.

I started off my 135-mile adventure with the goal of finishing under forty-eight hours. I had never run over 100 miles all at once. I had never run in 124 degrees. And I had never gone over twenty-eight hours without sleeping. It was uncharted territory for me. Yet, here I was, pushing myself to a forty-eight-hour non-stop finish with 13,000 elevation gain.

My other goal was to provide the kids at Boys Town Nevada a reason to be proud. I was raising money for their incredible organization. I didn't want them to be disappointed in the runner who was representing them. I wanted to go the distance for those kids. And finally, I wanted my crew to be proud. I wanted them to experience the finish line like I had one year before when I crewed and paced at

Badwater for Bill. My crew was the best and deserved a finish.

Bailey was my crew chief. I raised some eyebrows choosing an 18-year-old to be in charge of my very life. But I was not blinded by a mother's love. Bailey and I were now experienced working with each other. She is intuitive and smart beyond her years. Plus, she gave me major comic relief like no other. The rest of the crew included Georganna, whom I had met at Rio Del Lago and had become a dear friend, as well as Brendan, John, and Jimmy. Justin Yurkanin was on board to film a documentary about my run.

Initially there was a lot of laughter, hilarity, and light-heartedness when we got together to plan the event. This would later turn into somberness, intense focus, quiet determination, and every range of human emotion. When there are seven people on a mission to accomplish something out of the ordinary, amazing things happen.

Bill was also invited to run Badwater. We were now dating long distance and had moved from friends to partners. I had been divorced for awhile and dating was new to me. Our relationship was changing. I was sensitive to the fact that I wanted to do this race on my own. I had just finished Marathon Des Sable, which was a challenge of epic proportion. Badwater was tougher and I was at a disadvantage being underweight and weak. My emotions were also out of whack. Bill was trying to be helpful, giving me advice about how he had completed the race the year before. But I had my crew and I needed to do it my own way. There was a tension in our relationship which was definitely due to my overwhelming fear. The possibility of failing to complete the race scared me to death. I also wanted to do this event my way. I didn't want anyone to think I was holding onto Bill's coattails or anyone else's, for that matter. I was also getting media attention in Las Vegas, which caused more tension. Bill and I were dating and did not have enough experience in our relationship to understand each other's needs, and our competitive natures were clashing. I was finding my own strength and independence, and I simply did not want his help or even his viewpoint. Bill did not understand my waffling moods, which made little sense to me as well. Up to that point, he was my mentor and friend and I had listened to his every word. Now we were involved in a relationship, and I suddenly did not want his counsel.

We were arguing about everything. Before the event, he suggested that we start out running Badwater together. I told him, "I want to run this event on my own. If I am going to fail, let me fail."

He replied, "I'm just trying to help you. I think you are going to go out too fast." I was frustrated and plagued with the fear of failing. The tension was building, and I honestly wondered if our relationship was going to last through the race. Bill was completely confused by my emotions, partly because I could not express myself rationally.

I focused on my race and my crew and put the relationship aside for the time being. My crew and I were the first group to arrive at race start at 5:15 a.m. I was pacing around trying to keep from feeling terrified. Well, that wasn't necessarily true. I went from terrified to elated, and then those two emotions flipped every ten seconds.

Bill arrived with his crew and we all hugged and chatted nervously. I was extremely tense, and when Bill once again suggested that we start running together, I found myself wanting to scream. It had nothing to do with not wanting to be with Bill. It had everything to do with wanting complete separation from everyone else—to simply run by myself. I didn't want anyone around me. I desperately wanted to get inside my head without distractions. I could not be a girlfriend at that moment. Bill finally realized by my facial expressions that I was beyond reason. He stopped talking and we waited for the countdown.

The race began at 6:00 a.m., and I ran out too fast. But I couldn't help it. I let myself go. I needed to burn off steam. I was tense beyond all measure.

I calmed my mind with the steady rhythm of running as I monitored the sunrise. I was elated that the race had finally started after the endless waiting. I was now running on the white line of Badwater. (The white line is literally the side line of the road where participants run because it's slightly cooler than the rest of the pavement.) I knew that the brutal heat was ahead. It felt surreal to be alongside some of the most talented athletes on the planet. I was humbled and privileged to be on that white line.

At 17 miles, I was approaching Furnace Creek. My crew was cautioning me to slow down. I had given them my mileage goal sheet and race plan, and we all had agreed to follow the plan. I followed their instructions and slowed down.

Between Furnace Creek and Stovepipe, heading towards the 40-mile mark, the heat began bearing down. My crew gave me ice that I stowed under my hat, in a bandanna around my neck, down my shirt sleeves, and in my running bra (a female running secret). Brendan periodically sprayed me all over with ice water. Georganna kept putting food in front of me. Justin, John, and Bailey kept flinging the ice. Every member of the team worked in perfect harmony to keep me moving. Sometimes it got so hot that I put a sponge up to my face and just held it there as I ran. It felt as if I had my hairdryer on full blast aimed at my face. The wind blew and the heat became more and more brutal.

I believed if I got to Stovepipe, the 40-mile mark, in decent shape, I could possibly finish the race. I based this belief on past Badwater race results, which revealed that many runners did not make it past Stovepipe.

While I ran along with my insides roasting and my shoes melting, I had time to ponder the origin of various landmarks: the Funeral Mountains, Furnace Creek, Stovepipe Wells, Badwater, and Death

Valley. Road signs read "Caution Extreme Heat." The recurring theme was daunting. I was miserably hot. I did a quick Molly check: no protruding bones, no debilitating injury, and I wasn't dying; I was just extremely uncomfortable. So I kept going, putting one foot in front of the other.

At Stovepipe my crew put a stake in the road to show that I was leaving the course for a break. At a nearby hotel, my crew had arranged for a room where I could take a 10-minute ice bath. I jumped in with all my clothes on. It actually didn't feel good. It was rather shocking and horrid, but it did cool me down and got my legs ready for the first climb of the race, 17 miles up Townes Pass, a 5000-foot elevation gain. When I was getting out of the ice bath, I was bummed to see a big swollen bump on my Achilles tendon. It was sore to the touch. It was too early in the race for injuries. It freaked me out but there wasn't anything I could do at the moment. I put back on my compression socks and ran back out into the heat.

As I was climbing up Townes Pass, Dean Karnazes came running up behind me. (I was in the 6:00 a.m. start and Dean was in the 10:00 a.m. start, four hours behind me.) He shouted, "Hey Molly, I've been trying to catch you all day!" I told him that I wanted that on a recording so I could play it back to family and friends. Dean Karnazes, one of the most talented and accomplished runners in history, was trying to catch Molly all day. I still crack up when I think about that moment.

At about 7:00 p.m. while trudging up the pass, I started to feel sick. My crew had been trying to keep me eating 200 calories an hour, but the last hour I couldn't keep anything down. That was when I started having problems. After the 50-mile mark, I threw up my guts on the side of the road and took a five-minute break. I actually felt better. I began to eat watermelon and blue chips and started to rehydrate again. At the top of Towns Pass I took a break and addressed the Achilles problem, which was bothering me more and more. John, a chiropractor on our crew, taped my ankle with Georganna's assistance and I kept moving as the sun was setting.

Just then Bill's crew car pulled up beside me. I was surprised to see Bill in the backseat. His crew explained that Bill's feet were full of blisters. They had staked out and were taking him for medical attention. I stuck my head in the car and said, "Buddy, I am so sorry about your feet. I am sure the medical people can get you back on course soon."

He looked depressed and said, "I am in agony. How are you doing?"

I told him I was doing okay. I reached in and touched hands with him briefly, wishing I could help. It was so hard for us to communicate. There was so much emotional intensity as each of us was physically and mentally pushing ourselves to the limit of human endurance. My emotions were all over the planet: happy, elated, miserable, hurting, and on top of that we were dating! I didn't know what to think as the car pulled away.

With my headlamp showing the way, I continued on up over Towns Pass then the long downhill into Panamint Springs, the 70-mile mark where, around midnight, I experienced my first deep exhaustion. It melted into my bones making my limbs weigh a thousand pounds. I took a break in the front seat of the car with the air conditioning on my face and my eyes closed. I really didn't want to go back out. I just wanted to crawl into a ball and have an eight-hour nap with a little blanket and fluffy pillow and a masseuse rubbing my feet and a little cocktail drink with a . . . Just then my crew chief jolted me awake from my two-second dream by hauling me out of that delightful van and my beautiful vision. As John began to pace me, we scanned the road for rattlesnakes and saw a couple of dead ones that cars had run over. So much for blankies and fluffy pillows. Now it was an 18-mile climb up to

Father Crowley Point, a never ending, long, dark haul. Did I say never ending? The sun started to rise when I got to the summit. At first I was happy for light, but then I realized that the heat was coming back.

At the top of the summit I stopped for "blister care." I didn't want to look at them because I knew they were getting bad, so Georganna taped them up and off I went. I was so happy to be running on flat road that I took off with new energy into Darwin and the 90-mile mark. But 20 miles later, I hit a wall. I was spent. I was hotter than the day before. I felt like I was having an out-of-body experience. I longed to sit in the van. I couldn't get a grip so I stopped on the side of the road and just sobbed. Bailey and half the crew had taken a break at Panamint. I was with John and Justin, crying like a baby on the side of the road. I later found out John texted Bailey and summoned her for help. I asked for my iPod, dried my tears, and started to put one foot in front of the other. My entire body was screaming in pain. I was one hundred percent miserable. I didn't want to continue. All I could think about was stopping. I had to ask myself, Molly, is anything broken? No. Are you having a heart attack? No. Are you in grave danger? No. Then you must move on and focus on all your friends and family who are waiting for you to

The Badwater 100-mile mark

complete this adventure. Bailey showed up and marched up to me. "Mom," she said, "I want you to watch my feet. I am going to get in front of you and pace. Let's move."

The last 20 miles was mind-numbing. It was an out and out gut check to the finish. Maybe others cruise through this and have a different system that works, but for me it took everything I had physically and mentally. I used every mind game I could think of, every motivation, every meditation, and every mantra. When I got to Lone Pine and started up the Whitney Portal, the 121-mile mark, I had been running forty hours without sleep. My body was bent sideways as I weaved down the road.

Bailey held my hand for a minute and told me how proud she was of me. She was trying to get my attention. I realized that I was leaning, unable to stand straight and falling asleep on my feet. Exhaustion was clouding my thinking. I was hallucinating and thought I saw frogs crossing the road. I asked the crew to let me lie down for a second. I completely crashed for ten minutes in the van. I woke up feeling like I could actually function. But now there were fire trucks screaming up and down the road, and rumors began circulating that the race was stopped. I had 14 miles to go straight up to the Whitney Portal.

We eventually learned that the finish line had been moved in four miles because of forest fires. We could all smell the smoke in the air.

Bill's crew car pulled up to me coming from the direction of the finish line. During the night I didn't see that Bill had gotten back on the course after his feet were bandaged. He had completed the race! Bill was again in the backseat. I leaned in and told all of them congratulations. I was so happy and the elation of that moment woke me up. I could tell Bill was exhausted. I told him I would see him back at the race headquarters. He was whisked away.

The finish line was the most beautiful sight on the planet. I held hands with my wonderful crew, who had worked their hearts out tirelessly for 45:09 hours over 131 miles. We all ran in together to the finish line. I am forever in their debt and forever grateful. I will never forget our journey through Death Valley.

The last four miles of the course were closed and trees were still smoldering from the fire. I had the option of going back the following day to do the last four miles but my race was officially over and my crew totally spent. Plus for me, I felt satisfied that I had accomplished the impossible, and I was at peace with a race that was bigger than me. Badwater is daunting . . . the biggest, baddest race on the planet. I feel like my crew and I were granted safe passage on those precious days, and I was happy to have the experience behind me.

Badwater Finish with Race Director Chris Kostman.

My Badwater documentary is online thanks to videographer Justin Yurkanin:
http://www.jyurkanin.com/video/badwater

CHAPTER 11

Running in New Zealand—Northburn 100

"Go to Heaven for the climate, Hell for the company."
—Mark Twain

WHAT HAPPENED TO Tuesday?

I'd departed Las Vegas on a Monday, flown through the night, and landed the next day in Queenstown, New Zealand. Except now it was Wednesday. The explanation was that we had crossed the International Date Line, but that didn't seem like a sufficient reason for Tuesday to simply disappear.

I had flown to the other side of the world at the invitation of Lisa Tamati, whom I had met during the Badwater race in 2009. Actually, we were not formally introduced. We were both standing at the awards presentation, when I noticed that her adorable skirt and top coordinated perfectly with her Badwater buckle. (Her feet also looked considerably better than mine after our epic 135-mile race.)

Northburn Station 100 is an exotic trek into the wilds of New Zealand. The race includes a daunting 26,000 feet in elevation gain. The only compensating factor is the 48-hour cutoff, which gives relatively slow runners, like myself, an opportunity to successfully complete the run.

From Queenstown, I took a 45-minute bus ride into Cromwell, the home of Northburn Station. There I found "The Shed," a picturesque cottage that held a sophisticated bar and dining room complete with its own label of incredible wine. The scene was idyllic: calm, beautiful weather and scenery. No snakes, no bears, no mountain lions, no cougars—only sheep, cows, and prickly Spaniards. Later, I'd be surprised by rain, hail, snow, and 80-mile-per-hour winds, but for now, I seemed to be in the perfect climate.

When the race began, I was spellbound by the majestic beauty of the country. I've heard golfers remark that one of the primary attractions of the game is the beautiful environment and scenery surrounding the courses on which they play. The same holds true for ultrarunning. New Zealand is a land of exotic rainforests, rolling hills with green pastures, and towering, cloud-enshrouded peaks. At the top of the first peak, I shouted into a stiff breeze, "This is sooo awesome!" The views were amazing. I felt like I was on the top of the world.

Then, 15 miles into the race, a gust of wind broadsided me without warning, knocking me off my feet. Crash Sheridan down again. In addition to the customary scraped and bleeding knees and elbows, a quick Molly check revealed that I had sprained my ankle. Damn! I stopped at a checkpoint to tape my Achilles, which had begun to throb. I knew the 100-mile distance was no longer an option. I was hoping to drag myself to a 50K (31 mile) completion. Game not over yet.

Five miles later, another gust knocked me off my feet a second time. I was shocked that New Zealand could have winds with this power. My only consolation was that there were no witnesses.

Then clouds began to descend. Thick billowing mists turned into a whiteout, and visibility went down to a few yards. It was like Merlin's "the breath of the dragon" from the movie Excalibur or a scene from Lord of the Rings. Alone in a strange land and entrapped by this thick fog, I did my best to fight off fear and panic. I was periodically reassured by the pole lines that marked the course. Since there were no clear paths on the top of the mountain, it would have been easy to get lost without the white poles stuck into the earth about 50 yards apart. I realized that they used these poles because normal race markers, like cones with arrows, would have blown away.

It reminded me of when I climbed Mt. Whitney, where directional poles mark the desired path. Getting lost on a mountaintop can be hazardous to your health.

Earlier, I had wondered why the poles were so close together. Smart thinking! The fog got so thick at the top of Northburn Station that I could barely see the silhouette of each pole as I ran past. I was ensconced in a thick, wet fog that was rolling in giant layers. I thought about my survival blanket tucked into my pack. If things got worse, I could be reduced to huddling inside my survival foil tucked into one of the many rock crevices until the weather cleared or help arrived.

The mist turned into rain, which turned to blowing sleet as I ascended the steep mountain trail. Suddenly I spied two shadowy figures. I had to do a double-take to ensure that this wasn't one of my hallucinations. Two medics were back-tracking the course checking on the condition of runners. The wind was blowing so hard that we could barely hear one another speak. Although I assured them that I was fine, they ordered me to continue following the pole lines (no kidding) until I reached their vehicle and to climb in and wait for them. One was wiping rain off his glasses as he asked if there were any runners behind me. I told them I hadn't seen anyone for hours since leaving the last checkpoint. With their radios squawking, they disappeared into the mist.

Soon I reached their vehicle and climbed in. It was nice to be out of the cold and wind, but fifteen minutes later, my muscles started feeling cramped and I began shivering. I pulled on my thermal top, leaned up to the front and cranked on the heat. Then I took the time to eat but found no water in their emergency vehicle. Great. Later, I saw three shapes moving towards the car. At first, they looked like little ghostly images coming out of the fog. It was so eerie that I took a couple of pictures.

The medics had another runner, and they all climbed into the car. They drove down to another opening in the fence where, more runners were huddled in cars. All runners at that point had been rounded up into emergency vehicles. They said the winds were forecast to get worse (was that possible?) and that we could continue only if we stuck together.

By now, my fellow runner sitting next to me in the back seat had finally stopped shivering. We both hesitated and instinctively assessed one another. Her face was bright red, and her hair stuck out in all directions. Realizing I had to have looked every bit as bad made me even colder. Summoning all of my determination, I blurted, "I'm going!" and reached for the door handle. I yanked the handle and shouldered the door, but it was no sooner open then Wham! The wind slammed it shut again. That made me pause. Was it a sign? A sign from God? The courage I had summoned a few seconds before blew out that open door like a loose piece of paper. We sat in silence weighing our options: Stay in the nice warm car and return with the medics for food, wine, and rest—OR—venture out in the freezing sleet to run for hours and hours.

Soon the emergency guys were ready to leave, and it was decision-making time. Out the door we went. They had a tub of water to refill bottles, but the water was so cold splashing over my hand that I decided dehydration was better than frostbitten fingers. The wind was blowing so hard that two of the medical workers had to physically push a runner onto the trail. I could barely put one foot in front of the other. All the while I wondered if a giant gust would come along and blow me off the mountain, never to be seen again.

This was the ultimate adventure. We descended as a group battling gusts of hurricane force. We couldn't hear each other speak. We just hunkered down and tried to keep our balance. We looked like staggering drunks in a hurry to reach the pub.

An hour later the rain hit, full-on bucket loads, and we were running in a flooded, muddy road. All of our clothing was soaking wet. Our shoes, ankles, and shins were covered in mud. The only way to keep our body temperatures up was to keep running, so that's what we did. Finally, three hours after the medics sent us on our way, we approached the end of the first loop, which was also the end of the 50K. Other runners, who were steadfastly determined to complete a second loop (100K/62 miles) or the third loop (100 miles) continued on. Not me. I was wiped out.

I was never so happy to finish a 50K in my life. I am in complete awe of the runners who made it further. It was an inspiring site. I headed to the medical tent, where the nurse said that my Achilles tendon could not have taken any more. Lisa Tamati and her mum, Isobel, sat with me in the medic tent as I told them the conditions on the course.

Isobel was my newly adopted mum. We had bonded immediately after my arrival in New Zealand. I had lost my own mom, MJ, two months earlier. Isobel was caring and mothering to all the runners and I loved her positive nature. Isobel told me that my friend Ray Sanchez, the other American runner, was lost out on the course. The race director had sent sweepers (designated runners that "sweep" the course for lost or stranded runners) out to look for him.

We later discovered that Ray had made a wrong turn, which cost him a first-place finish in the race. Wrong Way Ray, a popular and incredibly fast runner, was known for his single-minded fast pace with his head down. He seemed to get lost in half of his race events. Otherwise, he usually came in first.

Terry Davis, the race director, had warned us at the race briefing about the unpredictable weather on the island, which can change within minutes. I thought carrying the required survival blanket and extra mandatory clothing was a bit of overkill until I was scrambling to pull them out when ascending the first peak. Mountaineering skills are a plus in this type of race. New Zealand's Kiwis are a hardy bunch. They are the most authentic, kind, and welcoming people. But don't let that fool you. Behind their easygoing nature, they are entertained by watching a bunch of naïve foreigners attempting to play in their backyard.

CHAPTER 12

Ancient Oaks . . . Madness!

*"If you start feeling good during an ultra, don't worry,
you'll get over it."*
—Gene Thibeault

IT WAS PAST midnight as I completed my 18th lap on the 3.46 mile loop in an enchanted forest near Titusville, Florida. I had been invited to the Ancient Oaks 100-mile race by ultramarathon runner Mike Melton. I thought I was losing my mind.

I had run in sandstorms in the Sahara Desert, through freezing fog and rain in the mountains of New Zealand, and under a 124-degree sun in Death Valley. Those and other races had been physically grueling, and each challenged me psychologically, but none of them affected me like Ancient Oaks.

Personally, I thought the enormous old oak at the corner of the Magnolia loop was to blame. I thought that big old oak chooses who she allows to complete that course, and she simply had something against me. Why else would I feel her taunting energy every time I passed her? She sat there like an immense Queen Bee with full reign over her enchanted forest.

The first time I saw her, I was astounded at her size and shape. She rose out of the ground like a huge creature with leaves so thick on her branches that she made a dense canopy that blocked out the sky. Her trunk was gnarly and knotted with shapes and crevices that resembled an old woman's face.

The Enchanted Forest is a dense mass of ferns, trees, and plant life so thick a person could get lost two feet off the path. The trails are leaf-laden carpets that weave through the jungle. Sunlight barely filters through the overhead canopy. Rare animals like feral pigs and armadillos come alive at night and unexpectedly jut out on the trail. There are snakes and spiders and unknown creatures that pop their eyeballs above the surface of murky waters. Old creaking bridges that cover the swampy sections are thick with moss.

When I first ran the course in 2009, I marveled at this secret garden paradise. I ran with my head whipping from side to side, astonished to see a million different shades of green. The vastness of the forest was mind-boggling. I felt like I was in a strange underworld far from civilization. Rounding the bend a mile from the start, I acknowledged the Queen and nodded my head as I ran by. She sat among her many servants: a dozen or so smaller oaks standing guard over their Queen in an area that local people call the Magnolia loop.

I approached Ancient Oaks confident and experienced. I had heard that it was a flat loop course and I expected an easy completion. The first year I made it 17 loops past the guard that year before I completely bombed out. Loop after loop through the tunnel of the oppressive overhanging branches, palms, and brush, I had an increasing feeling of claustrophobia and my energy seemed to be sucked out of me. It was disarming to me to pass my car in the parking lot every loop. That meant my car was calling me 29 times with its comfortable cushion seats and the smell of safety and rest. The trick was not to be pulled into the extreme desire to wrap myself in warmth from the damp and chill night dew at 2:00 a.m. The overwhelming mental war to overcome the desire for comfort versus the desire to finish was more intense than I had imagined. In a point-to-point race, I mentally reason that I am headed in the direction of home, but it is quite the opposite at Ancient Oaks. My mind wanted to stop and stay at the car every time I passed it, and I had to battle this thought constantly. My mind was screaming at me to stop every time my car came into view. As my body was wearing down, my mental power weakened, and I found myself drowning in a sea of psychological warfare.

Sixty other runners were in the race, but the forest is so thick and winding that the journey was solitary. Every now and then a faster runner would pass me, but for the most part I was on my own. The success rate is only 50 percent. During the course of the day and night, the number of runners passing me dwindled, and it became more and more lonely on that trail.

That first year I finally surrendered after dizziness and exhaustion set in. My mental toughness was broken by the Queen and her minions. Queen 1, Molly zero.

In 2010, I returned. How was I ever going to get to the full 29 loops with that big old oak blocking my efforts? I decided to make peace with the Queen. On my first loop I patted her trunk and said hello. I tried to be friendly and asked for safe passage through her forest. She seemed quiet and content. That night, however, a torrential rainstorm broke over me, and buckets of water unloaded from the sky. No stars could penetrate the thickness of the storm clouds. It was the wettest night I had ever experienced. The water poured in under my raingear. In that strange forest, it seemed that the laws of nature did not apply. In those pitch-dark midnight hours with my weak headlamp cutting out a triangle of light, the rain defied gravity and went sideways up my shirtsleeves. It poured up from the ground, sliding up my legs instead of down. Every inch of me was drenched to the skin. My soaked running shoes had the sensation of stepping into a bucket of water with every step. Water poured off the brim of my hat and down my neck. I approached a dense area of the loop and gasped as a giant armadillo almost tripped me as it scurried into my headlamp sloshing through the rain. The armored tank stared with beady eyes as I startled him to a standstill. We were both glued to the spot for a frightened second before he made the first move and dashed into the forest. All the night creatures seemed to be running wildly about as I ran through their paths and upset their quiet solitude. The pigs were making the most racket as I disturbed a mother and her piglets taking shelter under some ferns. I tried to be respectful on my journey through those slippery paths, but the branches seemed to pull my hair, and I had hallucinations of fairies grabbing and plucking at my running clothes. I'd turn to see what branch had tugged at me but nothing seemed close enough. Was I going mad? I made it 17 loops then bombed out, exhausted and beat after 60 miles. Queen 2, Molly zero.

In 2011, I returned with a new game plan. I wasn't going to touch her trunk or say hello. I was just going to slip in there, run, and then split before the Queen even knew I was there. I felt sick the whole race. I threw up my guts for hours, raining out puke on the ferns until it turned to dry heaving. Completely bombed out at 18 loops, I went home. Queen 3, Molly zero.

In 2012, I came back with a vengeance. I had a new game plan. I marched right up to that old oak on my first loop of the course. I stood at the bottom of her throne and said, "Hey Queenie, it's just you and me. Bring it on!" I wasn't going to take any shit from her. I paid my dues the last three years. I'd had it. I decided to throw some of my positive chanting and high energy into that forest during my run. I started each lap with joy and looked around at the beautiful plants and foliage. I appreciated the exotic ferns and moss-covered bridges that all the runners travel on over and over as they are making their way through the loops in the forest. I marveled at the birds and muffled sounds of the insects and hidden creatures. I loved that trail and felt great all day and into the night. Then, just after the sun set, my toe caught on a root, and I took a spill. That was not unusual for me. After an unusually massive fall, a group of running friends dubbed me "Crash," then "Crash Sheridan." But this fall hurt, and my ankle felt stiff. After walking on it for a while, I soon resumed at a slower pace. It still ached but not too badly. Game on. I knew old Queenie was awake and watching.

I made it to the 17th lap, then 18, then 19, the longest distance completed by me in that event. Ten laps to go! I decided to go all out and run harder before that old broad noticed I was beating her. Twenty loops down, but after running hard my ankle was screaming. Twenty-one loops . . . slow, slow, slow, 22 loops. My ankle was shooting stabbing pains up my leg at every step and getting worse. My time was slipping. The 23rd loop began with a giant six-foot rat snake blocking the trail. It might as well have been a boa constrictor. The whole body of the snake stretched across my path, and the last section of it was hidden in the trees.

Stu Gleman, ultrarunner and the original race director for Ancient Oaks, ran up beside me. "Don't worry," Stu said smiling. "That rat snake isn't poisonous, but watch out because it does have a vicious bite!"

I watched Stu as he stepped gingerly over it. I stood still wondering how long that snake would take before it moved along its merry way. It looked over at me and slowly coiled as if to strike.

Stu said, "Come on. Just jump it."

I shook my head, wondering if the rat snake could sense that I was injured. Stu finally convinced me to go around the back of it. As I limped behind it, Stu looked down at the leg I was dragging and asked what was wrong. I told him that I thought maybe the tendon was pulled, secretly wondering if my foot was broken, my eyes never leaving the snake as I maneuvered behind it. Safely past the predator, Stu encouraged me to keep going. After wishing me luck, I watched Stu run ahead and disappear into the plant life.

I continued to step and drag my foot, which was now in agony. The realization had set in that I would risk a worse injury and a longer recovery, placing my other racing events in jeopardy, if I continued. I bowed to the Queen at 25 laps, a total of 86.5 miles completed. I was 13.5 miles short of my 100-mile finish. Checkmate. Queen 4, Molly zero.

Of all my races, Ancient Oaks has been the toughest, mind-numbing chess game I've ever played. Am I mad to continue to go up against the Queen year after year? Maybe so . . . but if I'm invited back, I'll have a new game plan. I am considering carrying my Dalai Lama prayer beads, wearing a rosary, and listening to African Women warrior drumbeats as I chant and pray my way through the Queen's territory. Some might call me mad. Along that fine line of madness is my desire to reach past my physical and mental limitations. I want to go beyond what I think is possible. Is there really a big Queen oak tree out there purposefully stopping my progress, or is it my own internal Queen telling me I can't make it? Whether she is in my head or out in nature, it makes no difference. I still need to overcome her.

Part II

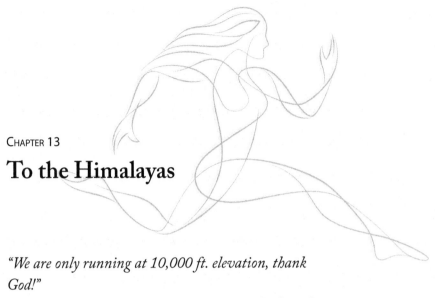

CHAPTER 13

To the Himalayas

"We are only running at 10,000 ft. elevation, thank God!"

—Rajesh Choudary, pacing Molly through Karu

SOMEWHERE AT THE end of the earth, between the borders of China and Pakistan, is a remote road in the Himalayas. This partially paved, dirt road is only open three months out of the year because the deep snow of the Himalayas restricts its use. Magically, the road opens for a short period of time and the rugged, colorful trucks from China bring their commerce into India. In the summer of 2010, this road became the setting for La Ultra, "The High," a 222 kilometer (138 mile) non-stop race through the mountains.

La Ultra was born from the imagination of Dr. Rajat Chauhan, visionary race director and runner. It is the highest, toughest ultra-marathon in the world.

After I finished the Badwater Ultramarathon, Rajat sent me an email congratulating me on my finish and asking if I would be interested in running his newly-created race. I immediately answered "Yes!" although I had no idea what the race would entail or exactly where the Himalayas were, for that matter. But I was fascinated by the idea of a grand adventure in such an exotic location.

Rajat's call came at the perfect time for me. I had just gotten back into a regular running schedule following weeks of recovery from Badwater. My feet had been totally trashed, including open wounds that were tender to the touch for days. I was also battling a little depression. Bailey and Taylor had left for college, and I missed their hilarity and fun. The empty nest syndrome was hitting full force. I had also hit the pinnacle of my ultrarunning goals at Badwater, and I was asking myself, what now?

Rajat's call filled me with excitement, primarily because the race had never before been attempted. Rajat also asked me if I knew any other experienced ultramarathon runners. Without asking, I knew Bill would be up for the challenge. Rajat informed me that two accomplished British ultrarunners had already agreed to run. So far there were four of us, but I knew that number would grow, and I was so glad I was involved from the start.

Little did I realize that the daunting logistics would discourage most runners from even considering the race. As Bill and I began to develop our plan of attack, we were emailing Rajat trying to gain an understanding of what was involved. It turned out that Rajat was still developing the course, and he was asking for our input. The race was to begin at 14,000 feet and head straight uphill for 26 miles to an 18,000-foot peak. When Rajat proposed crossing a second 18,000-foot peak, Khardung La, my response was, "Why not?" We were testing human endurance, so my thought was that we might as well go for it.

Bill remarked, "Oh, no," when he heard that Rajat had thrown in a second peak of 18,000 feet. "Rajat just made an extremely tough race impossible.". I don't know if I was being naive, stubborn, or just unrealistic, but I was excited. I wasn't thinking about what it would take physically to actually finish the race. To me, it was all about making the attempt. I wanted to see how far I could make it.

During this time, Bill and I had jumped to a new level in our relationship. Our friendship coupled with our adventures together had turned our partnership into a full-fledged love affair. Bill still lived in Reno working full time at Sierra Sciences, while I had settled into a smaller home in Las Vegas. Bill and I often met for long weekends of running adventures. I was completely fascinated with him. I never got tired of running behind him if only to check out his incredible calf muscles that, in my humble opinion, should be bronzed and put into the Smithsonian. I also admired his brilliant mind, although I didn't always understand his logical thinking. Sometimes I just shook my head in bewilderment at his intensity when mapping out our course for a weekend run or when he got frustrated at our conversations because I was ambiguous in a response to a question. He was meticulous to a thousand decimal places in his calculations and sometimes in his conversations. One time he showed me some calculations and graphs on his computer for a gene analysis. I told him that my brain was going to explode if I had to keep looking at that. His numbers and graphs were like a foreign language to me, and I marveled that anyone could comprehend them. Bill and I viewed the world from polar opposite perspectives, which seemed to draw us together and act as a barrier at the same time. He was kind and caring, yet complex. I loved our adventures, and I was looking forward to going to India together.

Part of the upcoming challenge was the extreme altitude. No mountain in the U.S. is comparable to a Himalayan peak of 18,000 feet. Mr. Whitney, the highest mountain in the continental U.S., is "only" 14,505 feet. Bill researched equipment, got a portable device for altitude adaption, and began experimenting. But that technological approach had no appeal for me. My plan was to get to India early, hang out for two weeks at altitude, and see how my body would adapt.

Before flying off for New Delhi, we received word from Rajat that he had received a letter from the Indian government informing him that it was humanly impossible for anyone to run 222 kilometers in the Himalayas at altitudes of 18,000 feet. I did not bother to tell my children, family, and friends about that little tidbit. I trusted Rajat and I trusted Bill. I felt I was in good hands. I had no expectations of the race itself. Was I scared? Yes. The undertaking was daunting. But I didn't let my mind wander into the fear zone. I was much more excited to experience India and the adventure. I did not want added pressure so I did not impose high expectations on myself. Since I had no idea if the race was humanly possible, and neither did anyone else, it was all an experiment. At the same time, I didn't consider myself a daredevil about to leap off to parts unknown. I had Rajat and Bill to accompany me. We were just heading off for one more ultramarathon. I had already completed, or at least attempted, fifty such races. What could go wrong?

Rajat, a fit runner who practices sports medicine, greeted us as we arrived at the New Delhi airport. Dressed in smart business clothes, he was younger than I had expected, probably in his late thirties. He spoke perfect English and I loved his accent. As soon as we walked out of the terminal, we were engulfed by the mass humanity of India. To say it was culture shock is an understatement. People were suddenly grabbing our bags and attempting to physically shove us into their selected cabs. Rajat gave sharp commands as his assistants grabbed our suitcases from the aggressive cabbies and escorted us to their private vehicles. The sights and sounds of New Delhi bombarded our senses. The destitution and poverty were shocking, the colors and exotic temples mesmerizing. We weaved through the streets packed with cars, motorcycles with four people crammed onto one seat, animals in the middle of the streets, naked babies on the sidewalk alone and crying, carts with hay pulled by donkeys in the middle of the road, and monkeys jumping onto the hood of our car. Bill and I stared with mouths agape. I thought of Dorothy in The Wizard of Oz, but the land we suddenly found ourselves in was far stranger than Oz.

But from the moment I stepped foot in that land, I felt a deep connection. I cannot explain it, but I was fascinated with India.

The next morning, after a quick tour of the Taj Mahal amid stifling, hot and humid temperatures, we flew to the distant town of Leh, deep in the Himalayas. Looking out the window of the airplane, the clouds parted and I had my first sighting of those magnificent mountains. I thought of the movie Shangri-La, when the passengers are hijacked on a plane and they look down at hundreds of snow-covered peaks, wondering where they are being taken. In the movie the plane crashes into giant snow drifts and they find their way to the magical city of Shangri-La, a place untouched by the world where no one ever grows old.

Our plane landed safely in a barren area surrounded by the massive Himalayas of Northern India. I felt exactly like we had crashed landed on the edge of the world. It was surreal to step off that plane and have the local Ladakhi people greet us with their ornate headdresses and colorful clothes. The locals put white silk scarves around our necks as a greeting. A couple of natives were playing instruments and dancing to welcome the tourists.

The mountains around us had snow at the tips but were so high that no vegetation grew near the top. We were already at 11,000 feet, higher than any U.S. airport. I was monitoring myself as I tentatively stepped from the plane and wondered if I would experience a headache or altitude symptoms of dizziness. We were greeted by Rajat's friends in Leh. The local cab drivers grabbed our luggage, threw it on the top of the tiny vans that looked like they would topple over, and we were whisked away to the town of Leh.

Leh was serene and quiet. It was definitely a Third World country, sitting precariously on the edge of the world, but there was a sense of peace there. The streets were dusty and dirty but there was order. I noticed the monks first—lots of them. Their red robes stood out as they walked through the streets among the villagers. We drove past temples and adorable wood and mud brick cottages that had ornate scrolled wood trim framing their windows. Up on the hillsides were several different monasteries carved into the mountainside.

We were brought to a small guesthouse near the center of town. A little garden patch framed the front entrance. Bill and I had rooms next to each other. I was glad to have the extra space to concentrate on the race and have quiet time if I needed it. As I stood there with bags in hand, Bill tossed his into his room, turned to me and pronounced, "I'm going up to Tang Lang La (18,000 feet) and see if this equipment works." He wheeled around to the cabbie, spoke a few words, and disappeared into the distance.

The other 18,000-foot peak we were scheduled to summit was Khardung La, one of the giant mountains surrounding Leh. Locals refer to the road as the highest motorable pass in the world. Paved at lower elevations, the road deteriorates at higher elevations. Freezing, flooding, and avalanches take their toll as crews work continuously to keep the road open for a few months in the summer.

We were told that we should spend a few days acclimating in Leh before attempting to breathe at 18,000 feet. Even then, it was recommended we stay at the top for no more than fifteen minutes. The altitude can affect people harshly. Dizziness, nausea, all the way to AMS (acute mountain sickness) that can cause death if not treated.

Knowing Bill as I do, I knew the scientist part of him was going to experiment with altitude immediately. Bill had already gone through the math, the pros and cons, and done hours of research. He used the equipment for six months before arriving in Leh. This was the moment that we both turned into endurance athletes. I was not about to turn into a nagging girlfriend telling him all the reasons I felt it wasn't smart to test the limits. He never made a decision lightly. I didn't necessarily agree and I was worried about him, but I also trusted his judgment.

I went into my room, opened up my little shutters, and looked out onto a valley filled with flowers, farmers' fields, and green trees, and a view of the most magical mountains in the world. I felt like I was in heaven, one of the few people to witness the massive Himalayas. I could see the colorful prayer flags flying from the tops of small homes in the distance. I was deeply moved and my heart was filled and fluttering like all those flags. I felt a deep connection to this place.

A short time later, I opened the door to find an Indian man with dark brown skin and a beautiful smile. Introducing himself as Neetu, he put his palms together and made a small bow. He said that Rajat had sent him over and asked if I would like a tour of Leh. Excited, I chirped, "Okay, let's go," as he led me to his motorcycle. I didn't bother to ask about a helmet because it was obvious I wasn't going to get one. We roared through the dusty streets of Leh, my arms wrapped around Neetu's waist, my hair flying wildly in the wind. He pointed to the market and shopping areas. He showed me the route to walk from the little guesthouse to the main parts of town. I was transfixed.

"Neetu," I asked, "can you take me to a monastery?" I was anxious to get inside a Buddhist monastery. The monks seemed so mysterious and exotic. I was curious about their culture and history.

"Which monastery do you want to visit?" asked Neetu. "There are seventeen monasteries in this region. It is a spiritual place. It is said that Leh is the only city where both Jesus and Buddha visited in their lifetime."

Without thinking, I shouted through the wind, "I want to go to any monastery!" Neetu turned the motorcycle sharply around, and we whipped past a cow roaming in the center of a street. We rode past townspeople with their traditional colorful Ladakhi clothes. The shopkeepers had their fruits and vegetables laid out on carts and blankets on the street. I saw foreigners and caught phrases of their conversations in German and French as we zipped by. During the trip I was surprised that I did not meet any Americans. In fact, I've never met another American in three subsequent visits.

Meanwhile, I did notice some effects of altitude. Both of my pens had exploded in my purse and I felt a wave of dizziness, but I was not about to curtail my exploration. Neetu pulled the motorcycle up outside an archway on the main street. He gestured for me to follow him through the doorway, which opened into a large court-yard. In the center stood a huge temple with a gold roof. Prayer flags were waving from the corners of the building. Monks were walk-ing around the perimeter of the temple spinning intricately carved wooden spools with their hands in honor of Buddha.

Following Neetu's example, I slipped off my shoes, crept up the steps, and entered the temple. A giant colorful statue of Bud-dha dominated the room. Beautiful tapestries hung on all the walls. Neetu whispered that the tapestries are thangkas, hand-painted by the monks, depicting a different Buddhist deity. Bright fabric framed the pictures. In the corner of the room sat a monk on a cushion.

Neetu gestured for me to approach. "He is the Lama of the temple."

And there he was, My Lama. . . .

CHAPTER 14

The Holy Man

*"You were born to be a player. You were meant to be
here. This moment is yours."*
—Herb Brooks

I HAD NO idea what the correct etiquette was for visiting a Buddhist
temple. Growing up Catholic, I had no idea if I was supposed to
genuflect, bow, or curtsy. I noticed that there were several local
townspeople that were prostrating themselves on the floor as they
worshiped Buddha in the center of the room. I stood there like an
ignorant foreigner that had just tracked mud through a beautiful
sacred dwelling.

The monk looked over at me with curiosity. I imagined that it was
not very often that a six-foot tall American blonde entered the temple.

I walked over and sat at the monk's feet, cross-legged as he was.
I put my palms together and bowed my head. "Hello," I murmured.

In a thick Indian accent he asked, "What is your name?"

I told him my name and said I was from Las Vegas.

He closed his eyes, tilted back his head, and said, "Ahhhh . . .
Vegas."

This proved it, I thought to myself—everyone in the world has
heard of Las Vegas. I wondered if he thought I was a sinner from
Sin City.

Lama Tsephel

He had the most perfect skin and intense brown eyes. He appeared petite wrapped in his red robes sitting on his pillows. I tried to figure out his age, but he had no lines in his face and I couldn't tell if he was thirty-five or fifty-five. He told me his name was Lama Tsephel. He asked me why I had come to Leh, and I found myself telling him all about the race and answering his many questions.

His English was fair. The language in Leh is Ladakhi. There are several different dialects in the region including Hindi and Urdu, which didn't really matter because I didn't understand any of them. I loved the melodic accents when the Lama spoke, even though I could not understand some of his phrases in English. The Lama reached out and touched my hand as I got up to go. "I will see you again," he said, and gave me a brilliant smile. I hugged him, then wondered if that was inappropriate. He didn't seem to mind. I followed Neetu's example and laid down several rupees at the altar of Buddha, waved to the Lama, and left feeling happy and peaceful.

Bill came back from Tang Lang La and his 18,000-foot experience and was absolutely ecstatic. He had gone to the top of the peak and ran successfully. It proved his theory that the Alto Lab system that he had been using for six months was working.

The next day, we had a race meeting with Rajat, who told us that Mark Cockbain was coming about four days later but that Sharon Gator, one of the British runners, withdrew because of an injury. So there would be only three of us running in this high altitude expedition. Crew members began to arrive and the teams started to assemble. Rajat had arranged support vehicles for each runner. The vehicles would follow us with two to three crew members on the road for the entire distance, providing food, our change of clothes, and general assistance. Most of the crew members were friends and relatives of Rajat. Some were experienced runners and others came along for the adventure. One of the most adorable crew members was Pramond, an Indian man who was a cousin of Rajat. Pramond looked like a football player that could rip your head off, but was a big, soft-spoken, gentle Indian man. Rajat assigned Pramond to me as my bodyguard. Since I was the only woman running the race in the Himalayas, he wanted me to have some sort of protection due to the fact that we had to go through military checkpoints in remote locations. Pramond spoke little English, but we understood each other and became fast friends.

After two days of acclimatizing in Leh, we made our first drive up to Khardung La. The road was harrowing—lots of trucks and vans barreling around corners, teetering on the edge of cliffs and stopping for landslides. On the positive side of things, the views were spectacular. We were driving up there in miniature vans at the same time giant, colorful trucks were coming through, so it got a little scary. The exhaust fumes from the trucks were huge black clouds that did not dissipate because of the altitude. So the exhaust just hangs in the air. I knew that was going to be an issue running the race. Having only 40 percent oxygen is bad enough, but breathing in toxic fumes on top of that was going to be a problem.

When we all arrived at the top of Khardung La that first day, I noticed the altitude difference immediately. When I got out of the car, I felt as if my veins were full of lead. I couldn't believe my energy had disappeared. There was a little tea-shack with a gift shop at the top of the peak where cars stop and tourists gather. I walked over and sat down to rest. Suddenly I noticed that something was causing quite a stir. More people were looking at me than the scenery. Soon strangers were approaching and asking to have their photos taken . . . with me. At first I thought maybe they thought I was someone famous. Then I was informed that they were taking my picture simply because I was a tall white person.

The top of Khardung La is covered in prayer flags. The Buddhists believe that the wind blowing through the prayer flag allows prayers to be answered. So there are thousands and thousands of colorful prayer flags on top of the snowy peak of Khardung La.

Looking out over the edge of the cliffs, down into the valley and over to hundreds of mountains in the distance, I wondered how in the world I was going to run this race. I couldn't imagine how I was going to get over the top of this mountain. I had ten more days to acclimate, and I knew I needed every single day.

Later on, we drove back down to the village of Leh, and a group of us got together at the guesthouse. We were chatting, talking about our day, and I noticed Pramond was nowhere to be seen. I asked Rajat, "Where is Pramond?"

Rajat put his hand on my shoulder and said, "Molly, Pramond started having altitude sickness this morning and we had to send him back to New Delhi."

Rajat, Mark, Bill and I acclimating at 18,000 ft., Khardung La

I was shocked. How did Pramond get sick so fast? Rajat explained that during the night, Pramond had trouble breathing and had a horrific headache. They took him down to the Leh hospital and he was diagnosed with acute altitude sickness. Pramond seemed like such a big, tough guy. Out of all the people that we were with, he was the least likely person to be affected by altitude. I was devastated to hear that he had succumbed and would not be with me. Rajat assured me that my two remaining crew members, Randy, a writer from Michigan, and Sindhu, an Indian runner from Bangalore, would be sufficient.

I had met Randy in Las Vegas when I was training for the Himalayas. He was in his sixties, had silver hair and a goatee, and told me he was a journalist for several magazine publications. He was standing at a rest stop area at Red Rock Canyon, outside Las Vegas, when I ran in to replenish my water. He came up to me with his notepad, explained that he was writing a story about Red Rock Canyon, and asked how far I was running.

"I am running the 13-mile loop," I explained. The loop is a rolling scenic drive that weaves through the canyon.

"You are running the entire loop?!" he exclaimed. I didn't bother to tell him that this was my low mileage day. "Have you ever done this before?!"

"Yesterday," I replied. I chatted with him for a few minutes longer and gave him my email information for follow-up.

Randy emailed me over the next several months and became intrigued with my Himalayan adventure. He told me that he wanted to come to India and join my crew. I warned him that crewing was difficult and I needed experienced individuals. I felt that he had an idealistic view of crewing. I tried to explain that crewing means you are stuck in a vehicle for hours on end serving a tired, sometimes cranky runner. This particular race was even more difficult than most. It hadn't been done before. The cutoff time was sixty hours, which meant little sleep or rest for three days in extreme weather and dangerous conditions. But Randy was insistent. Finally, I relented and referred him to Rajat. That was a big mistake. Randy ended up on my crew, and I have no one to blame for that but myself.

Sindhu, my other crew member, was an Indian woman who was a friend of Rajat's. A runner herself, Sindhu knew what was needed and worked efficiently. I was thrilled to have a woman on my crew.

For two weeks before the race I lived an idyllic life. Every morning in my little room, I opened my shutters and looked out at the snow-capped mountains. Every other day, I travelled up to 18,000 feet for a little bit longer to acclimate. I began to plan for the race. At times I would sit with Bill, Rajat, and Mark to talk about the supplies we would need. At other times I escaped to go off by myself and get my mental game plan in place. It was overwhelming for me to think about running the entire distance. Therefore, my mental plan was to run each section separately. It somehow made the idea of the run more realistic and doable when I broke it down to smaller pieces.

Rajat had Jitin and Abhijit, his main team members, in charge of the logistics of vehicles, supplies, and crew. Jitin, who would be my driver during the race, had driven his personal vehicle all the way from New Delhi to use as a crew vehicle.

Over the two weeks leading up to the race, I fell in love with the town of Leh and the people. I loved seeing the cows walking aimlessly in the streets. I loved looking at the colorful red robes of the lamas. I loved the people, who were always so nice and polite.

I missed my kids back home, but I was able to occasionally shoot off an email at the Internet Café in town, although sometimes the Internet was down for days on end. It was completely unpredictable. Electricity was sporadic in town, too. My room had a small shower and toilet but hot water was intermittent. Usually if there was any hot water at all, I quickly filled a bucket and had a sponge bath. Attempting a shower was risky because freezing glacial water could shoot out of the faucet at any moment. There are no Laundromats in Leh. All clothes are hand-washed. The bucket in my bathroom had the dual use of sponge bath and clothes washer. After hand washing my clothes, I hung them on the clothesline at the roof of the guesthouse. They were not as pretty as the prayer flags blowing in the breeze.

The time arrived, and we prepared to depart. In two days, we were going to drive from Leh to Khardung Village, where we were going to camp for two additional days before the start of the race. I put all my affairs in order. I went down to the little Internet Café, and I sent off emails to my dad, my sisters and brothers, daughters, son, nieces—I told everyone that I was excited and ready. I did not share my fear, not even with myself. I rode the wave of excitement and adventure. Devin, Bailey, and Taylor, and my sister Colleen sent me inspiring messages that carried me during those weeks. I had my foundation of support securely surrounding me. I felt incredibly free. I couldn't imagine any place on earth that I would rather be than in India, at that moment in time, on the edge of the world, the most incredible journey of my life.

I had visited Lama Tsephel almost every day during my time in Leh. He radiated energy, a peace and calmness that was palpable. Each time I left him he would say, "I will see you again." Then he would flash that big smile. I always thought his comment was odd because the race would end in the Morey Plains, and we would drive from there back to New Delhi, several hundred miles to the south.

Before we left Leh, I took Bill, Mark Cockbain, and all our crews to meet Lama Tsephel for a group blessing. With all the frantic packing and preparations for the race, I thought a trip to the monastery would be a pleasant distraction.

Upon our arrival, we were informed that Lama Tsephel was not due to be at the monastery that day. Realizing that I would not see him again, I was totally bummed. As we were all piling out of the temple, Lama Tsephel appeared as if he were an apparition. He said in his broken English, "Hello, I am not here today, but I know you come. I would see you again."

He gestured for us to stand next to Buddha and began to chant and tied a red cord around each of our wrists. After the Lama prayed over us, we presented him with an honorary crew T-shirt. I also gave the Lama some inspirational sayings given to me by my dear friend Jane and my other girlfriends (The Posse) before I left for India. They had all written inspirational sayings and wrapped them in a precious little package. I shared them with the Lama in thanks for blessing us. The Lama grasped my hand when I was leaving, thanked me, and told me that he was leaving tomorrow to see His Holiness, the Dalai

Lama in Dharamsala. He wanted to know if Bill and I would be traveling through the city, but I told him that Bill and I were leaving and I would not be seeing him again this trip. The Lama looked at me and holding my hands, he said, "I will see you again." I thought he was confused, but I was honored by his comment. He kept saying, "I will see you again." Then we parted. I felt like crying.

The next day, as we packed and got everything together to leave Leh, panic hit. Everything hurt. My body ached; my muscles were tense. I knew it was stress. I was suddenly scared. I started praying to Buddha, Jesus, God, the Green Tara, all the Hindi Gods, Mary, Joseph, the angels, saints, and the Lama. I was asking for someone to watch over me and lend the helping hand I would surely need—whoever is up there. I lay in my bed taking deep breaths and telling myself that I needed to get a grip and just focus. I hoped Lama Tsephel was praying hard.

I sensed the biggest running adventure of my life would become a death-defying act. Had my previous long distance runs prepared me for the grandest run of them all? Or had I run headlong into much more than I was physically and emotionally prepared to tackle? I instantly knew I'd be calling on powers deep within myself that had, until now, been untested.

CHAPTER 15

Mayhem at the Border

"Know the rules well so you can break them effectively."

—His Holiness The Dalai Lama

WE HAD ABOUT forty people on the expedition. The plan was to drive several hours to Khardung Village on the other side of Khardung La. We would camp at 14,000 feet and begin the race the following day. I would be riding in the car with my crew, Randy, Sindhu, and Rajesh, whom Rajat had added to my crew at the last minute to replace Pramond. Mark and Bill would be riding separately with their crews, and Rajat's car would bring up the rear.

The last couple of days before our departure, Bill had not been himself. He was tired and had a raspy voice and cough. He was taking a lot of naps and thought he was catching a cold. We didn't think it was altitude sickness symptoms, but I was worried because he seemed to be getting worse.

Right before we climbed into the cars to head out, Rajat took one last look at Bill and made the decision to take him to the hospital to get checked out. He told me to head to the camp at Khardung Village and wait for him there. Bill came over, hugged me, and told me not to worry, but he looked awful. He told me he would meet me at camp. I kissed him good-bye, put on a brave face, got in the car, and started crying. This is not how I wanted to start the race. I was a nervous wreck already, and now I was worried about Bill. The race hadn't even started, and I realized that one of the toughest parts of this event was getting to the start line.

As Rajat drove off with Bill in one direction, we departed the opposite way on the long road to Khardung La. My heart ached for Bill. We got separated from Mark's vehicle early on and found ourselves with a quiet that settled on us like a heavy blanket. Bill's departure was an unexpected and devastating turn of events. Sindhu, sensing my distress, put her hand on my shoulder and attempted to comfort me. There was nothing anyone could say. I resolved to keep moving forward, hoping that Bill would show up in camp by nightfall.

We were in the middle of nowhere with rarely a human being in sight. Every now and then we would see a yak. We were climbing up and over the huge pass for hours. It was hard to imagine that I would be running all of this in a couple of days. I spied a tiny tea stall on the side of the road and asked Jitin to stop. (Actually, I had to go to the bathroom.)

When I got out of the car, who do I see? Lama Tsephel. In the middle of nowhere. I had to blink twice. Is this really the Lama? He walked over and said, "I told you I would see you again." I asked what he was doing there. He said, "I am on my way to see His Holiness, the Dalai Lama." I looked over and spotted a partially hidden car on the other side of the tea stall. Just by coincidence we had stopped at the same place, at the same time, on the same day. I hugged him and told him what happened to Bill. He said he would send prayers to Bill.

When I turned to go, Lama Tsephel said, "I will see you again." I believed him this time.

Later that afternoon, we came upon a military checkpoint. A soldier came up to our car with his big gun and asked for our papers. A crowd of men who were milling around the checkpoint began looking at our car, making angry gestures, and pointing at me. Meanwhile, the solider posed all sorts of questions to Jitin. The two of them were talking in Hindi, so I didn't understand what was being said. Suddenly the angry crowd approached our car, and voices were raised. The crowd was growing, and it seemed like there was some big misunderstanding. I sat in the back seat with Sindhu trying to act inconspicuous. Rajesh, my pacer, decided to get out of the car to clear things up. In response, one of the men punched Rajesh in the face. Suddenly the fight was on and people were screaming. Pandemonium. Angry, screaming, fighting men. Jitin was yelling at us, "Stay in the car! Stay in the car!" More military men began showing up with their guns drawn, pointing at the car. I thought about taking a photo, but that might provoke more anger. Then an officer, who looked like he was in charge, marched up and told everybody to shut up. Then he ordered us to hand over our passports.

Randy, the journalist, panicked and yelled, "Molly don't give him your passport. They will put us in a prison."

I calmly replied, "Randy, we are giving him our passports because he is the military authority, and we don't have a choice." I was annoyed with Randy but I also understood his fear. I was afraid myself. I still didn't understand what the problem was. We couldn't understand what we had done wrong. After handing our passports to the officer, he turned and barked orders to the crowd. Jitin, Rajesh, and everyone else disappeared into a building. Meanwhile, Randy, Sindhu, and I sat in silence wondering what was going to happen. Our minds were full of thoughts like, how bad can it get? Are we in a place we aren't supposed to be? Don't we have permits? I was petrified. I didn't want to discover what a military prison was like on the border of China and Pakistan.

After a good half hour, the military officers came out of the building followed by the angry men and walked straight to the car.

Men were pointing at me and raising their voices. One tried to open the door where I was sitting, obviously in an effort to draft me out of the car. It was so unnerving. Again, voices were raised and again there was a surge of indiscernible shouting as two men continued to yank at my locked car door. I thought again about lifting my camera out of my backpack, but I was too frightened. It was surreal watching the angry men pushing and shoving one another from inside the safety of the car.

I was fairly sure the problem revolved around the fact that I was a white woman who was not supposed to be where we were, but I didn't know why. The shouting men kept pointing at me and screaming in Hindi. I imagined they were saying something like, "Off with her head!" I decided not to raise the level of rage by snapping a photo. I thought about later examining such a photograph in the comfort of my home. In my mind it was a National Geographic photo-op, the kind that gets the honor of the cover of the magazine. An average person flipping through the stack of magazines at their mundane doctor appointment would have seen that photo and grabbed it up to take another look. They would be in awe wondering if it was a photo of a lynch mob or political uprising. They probably would have wondered if the person taking the picture had survived the onslaught. All those random thoughts sped through my mind as if I were not really there. My consciousness did not want to register the extreme danger of the situation. I had to place my feet firmly on the floor of the car to steady myself and retain some semblance of calm. I did not want to be consumed with the fear that was wrapping its cold claws around me squeezing my reason and logic away.

Jitin reappeared out of the military building and walked slowly towards the car with a military officer, who appeared to be high ranking with a special sash and adornment on his coat. He seemed to demand respect as he barked instructions and vehemently made motions to Jitin as they made their way through the angry men. Jitin looked pale and had his eyes downcast. He and Rajesh climbed into the front seat as the military officer shouted instructions. A hush dropped over the crowd.

The military officer returned our passports, then nodded to Jitin, who started the engine and slowly pulled away from the scene. There was complete silence in the car. The angry men continued to stare at us, but slowly began to disperse.

"What is happening!?" I burst out. "Rajesh are you okay?" I looked over at the red whelp where Rajesh had been hit. Rajesh was rubbing his face but no one said a word. We continued to drive quietly for a few minutes. I looked at everyone's serious, scared faces. The tension in the car was as taut as a wire ready to snap. Finally, Jitin broke the silence and explained what had transpired.

"The cab drivers think we have stolen their business," he quietly explained in his thick melodic Indian accent. "They are union workers who drive tourists through the Himalayas for a short three months out of the year. It is their only income." He spoke quietly as if he didn't want to break the precious moment of calm, his eyes nervously darting back and forth in the rearview mirror for any signs of pursuit.

"These workers have watched us going up and down the mountains over the last two weeks. They see that you are white. They see my car, which does not belong here, and they know I am not in their union. They believe I have moved into their territory and stolen their business." He looked over at Rajesh with a worried expression on his face and asked about his injury in Hindi.

Āpa kaisē haiṁ?

(How is your face?)

"Acchā," Rajesh replied. "Vaha ēka baccē kī taraha mārā."

(I am okay. He hit like a baby.)

The union cab drivers, who drive small miniature vans that do not resemble a cab in any way, did not know that Jitin drove his car up from New Delhi, a private citizen, in order to simply help Rajat Chauhan, the race director, drive the runners to the race start. Later on, we found out that the military had initially sided with the union in the giant scuffle at the border. The military was ready to throw us all in prison. But promises were made and maybe money was exchanged. They grudgingly let us continue for the time being. Rajat later met with the military and the union and ironed out the problems. The solution was to hire the cab drivers and their small little vans to drive runners and crew throughout the race, which remains the situation to this day. But that first year, as a small group of adventurers were trying to accomplish something that had never before attempted, we stumbled into a society full of suspicion and fear. I came to find out that Pakistan, China, and India distrust one another intensely. There is constant turmoil as to where the borders begin and end and who owns what land, which has persisted for centuries. We were attempting to tread lightly on that thin border between three volatile countries, but we had little knowledge of local customs and traditions. From their perspective, we were foreigners possibly taking advantage of the locals.

Rajat turned out to be an incredible diplomat. He routinely met with military and union officials to make our passage through those remote and barren areas as safe as possible. It was ironic that we were attempting to lift the human spirit with an endeavor of great physical endurance surrounded by temples, monks, and the Dalai Lama, yet we had to deal with the other reality of fierce military borders, guns, and countries accustomed to war.

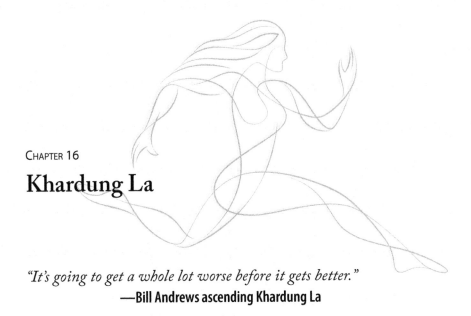

Chapter 16

Khardung La

"It's going to get a whole lot worse before it gets better."
—Bill Andrews ascending Khardung La

AFTER THE SOBERING border incident, we continued to wind our way through gigantic mountains, canyons, and valleys sunk deep in the Himalayas towards Khardung Village. All the while I was realizing that I would be running along these roads all the way back to Leh and over to the Morey Plains. The rocky roads were full of ruts and at points dropped off to sheer cliffs with barely enough room for a car to pass. Every now and then a massive Chinese truck would come along and demand, simply by its size, that we hug the cliff so it could pass. I had to bring my arm in from the window in order to keep it from being hit by the passing trucks. A few times we had to stop our vehicle so snowplows could clear an avalanche area where the constantly melting snow would slough off the mountaintop. Neetu had warned me that the roads get quite flooded late in the afternoon as the sun heats up and melts the snowy peaks. I knew that I would be running through water and snow during the race even though it was late summer.

Rounding a bend, I got my first glimpse of Khardung Village, population about fifty . . . maybe. It was a glorious area. It seemed that all the snows and waters of the surrounding peaks washed down into Khardung Village, making it a green and fertile valley. It sat there amid these enormous mountains with yaks and goats gently grazing in the fields, mud huts with grass roofs sporadically dotting the landscape.

We drove into a dirt driveway up to one of the huts, where two naked babies were sitting in a tub of water outside the door. A mother with bright scarves wrapped around her head and face was busy washing them as they squealed in the water. She looked up at our car and pointed for us to pull to the side of the house. As we parked we could see twenty tents behind her house, where Rajat's team had made camp in the field. All of this for only three runners. (The expedition was comprised of teams to oversee the runners' safety, the cooks, the logistic experts, the drivers, and the staff.)

I made my way to my tent that was shown to me by the Ladakhi guides, and I hurriedly threw my belongings inside so I could take a moment and breathe in the air and watch the clouds floating over the magnificent peaks. I felt like I belonged there. I had an overwhelming sensation of gratitude that I was able to experience the sight and sounds of the Himalayas. I was standing in a dream. Soon I lay on a blanket outside my tent, closed my eyes, and took deep breaths. I was tired from the drama of the border and was wondering what became of the others. I was hoping they didn't have similar frightening experiences.

Several hours later, I heard an engine and opened my eyes to find Bill and Rajat climbing out of their vehicle. Relief washed over me.

I ran up to Bill and hugged him so hard. He explained that the doctors gave him a checkup at the hospital and said he could run. His voice was still raspy and he looked tired to me, but he had no signs of altitude sickness.

Rajat had followed up with the military and paid additional permits for our safe passage. Everyone else safely reported to the camp. They were all grateful they hadn't had a tall blonde woman in their car.

After everyone was safely at camp, Bill and I walked over to a tiny outdoor tea stall in the village. Several people from our expedition were sitting around a little plastic table with chipped chairs. A red checkered tablecloth covered the plastic tabletop and a simple canvas tarp covered the seating area next to the stall. We were surrounded by spectacular views of the Himalayas. In any other country with such magnificent views, we would have been in a bustling tourist town, similar to the Swiss Alps, full of shops and businesses. Instead, because of our remote location, a brown-skinned woman with a colorful scarf wrapped around her head and a long brown dress belted with a bright fabric served us tea in little round cups with no handles. Bill's crew was there, including Nischal and Sabine, two hilariously funny women who were friends of Rajat's and belonged to a running group in Bangalore. Sabine was German and had married an Indian man and settled in India. Nischal was engaged to be married when she returned from the expedition and was in the middle of describing her future mother-in-law when we walked up to the stall. Everyone was laughing at whatever she had just said.

Nischal and Sabine had been instrumental in helping me adapt to culture in India. The first day I arrived in New Delhi, they both invited me to go sightseeing and shopping at the market. I opened the front door to greet them in my cute skort and top. They both looked at my outfit, then looked at each other, then back at me.

"You can't wear that in public, Molly," Sabine shook her head.

"What?!" I looked at both of them not understanding. They were wearing similar bright T-shirts and capri pants that hit mid-calf.

"They will call you a slut at the market," Nischal laughed. "The men will not keep their hands off you. Your skirt is too short!"

"Are you serious? Come on, really? I am an American, I'm not a native here. Anyway, this is not a skirt, it's a skort and has shorts underneath." I lifted the shirt and showed them the little shorts under. "I've seen other Americans in shorts and skirts!" I reasoned.

"Nevertheless, the men here will be touching you and groping, which is very distracting while shopping. Everyone will label you a prostitute!" Apparently, my outfit would confirm everyone's suspicion about a woman from Las Vegas.

"Oh, for God's sake. It's 100 degrees outside and 100% humidity!" I switched my skort, which I did not believe was that short, for modest capri pants and monitored the sweat beads that rolled down my back the rest of the day.

I was missing the heat and humidity of New Delhi as we sat there in Khardung Village. The sun was sinking and a chill hit the air. The cold at 14,000 feet in August was remarkable. Warm days and frigid temps at night.

Mark joined us at the tea stall, and we all sat watching the sun slowly set in the field. Abhijit, Rajat's right-hand man and logistics partner for the race, leaned over in his chair to speak Hindi to the brown-skinned woman pouring our tea. She seemed to understand Hindi well enough even though the townspeople spoke Ladakhi. She nodded to Abhijit, hurried over to her stand, and brought back little biscuits for us to eat with our tea. She kept smiling and bowing at us, delighted to have so many customers.

"I have a question for everyone," Bill announced as our little group turned all eyes on him. I was so happy he was feeling better and the health scare had passed.

"Why isn't there toilet paper in India?"

Mark replied, "Toilet paper? There aren't any toilets! Why would you need the paper?"

Everyone laughed. There certainly were not any toilets in this place. Or running water. The townspeople maintained small grass huts (outhouses) behind their clay brick houses. Within was a hole in the ground where one squatted and did her (or his) business. Mini tents with their own hole served as our restrooms. Otherwise, if we felt the call of nature, we had to find a tree or large rock to hide behind. Too few restrooms is a common problem in ultrarunning. I always carried a packet of tissues.

Bill looked around at the dusty street with two huts and asked, "Do you guys think there are any toilets around here?"

More outbursts of wild laughter. There was no way we were going to see a toilet for weeks. I think it may have been a release of nervous tension because I couldn't stop laughing. Suddenly we all collapsed into hysterics. All the pent-up fear and anxiety came pouring out. Tears were streaming down my face. The harder I laughed, the more everyone around me joined in. It was a wave of infectious laughter that went on for ten minutes until my face ached from the exertion.

Bill stood up and announced with all seriousness, "Now I have to go."

More laughter. Fits of laughter. Bill sauntered down the street looking for the elusive toilet.

The temperatures plummeted as the sun set behind the mountains, and we all made our way back to the tents. By now I was freezing, so I quickly slid inside my tent and zipped myself in. Bill and I, now in our competitive race mode, had separate tents even though we were a couple.

I went over the game plan in my head, which was simply to keep moving. It never entered my head about what place I would finish. The guys were both stronger. Mark was almost twenty years younger. There was no reason for me to compare myself or stress over my upcoming third place finish. My physical gifts never lay in my speed. But I did know that through experience in many distance races that I had outlasted runners with greater gifts than me simply because of my mental strength. Ultramarathons are all about summoning the mental strength and determination to keep going while every cell in your body screams in pain and agony.

I slept fitfully. My mind kept returning to the race as my stomach churned with knots of tension. The next day was more of the same. I went over all my gear with my crew. Jitin had been replaced with a local Indian cab driver so we wouldn't all be thrown in prison.

I felt tired. I hadn't eaten well in the two weeks I had been in India. I could not eat the curry. The curry spices worked havoc on my stomach and everything had curry in it. I lost close to eight pounds since I had arrived, and I didn't have eight pounds to lose. While I watched everyone else clean their plates and return for seconds, I forced down a few spoonfuls of rice and some pieces of roti (Indian bread).

I found myself walking alone through the meadows to take my mind off the race. I just wanted to start the race. Out on the course, I would be moving instead of lying around thinking about the race.

On the morning of the race, we all rose at 4:00 a.m. It was freezing cold. While the crew and drivers were chatting and buzzing around the camp with last minute gear check and packing, Bill, Mark, and I were quietly trying to eat and mentally prepare for the day.

Bill still had his raspy voice, but otherwise he seemed okay. Mark was always quiet so it was hard to discern his mindset. I didn't want my picture taken, which everyone was trying to do, and I didn't really feel like talking to anyone although I faked it because I didn't want to be a stressed-out pain in the ass. Everyone around me was working hard to set us up for success, and I didn't want to bring anyone down with a negative attitude.

From Khardung Village we all loaded into the cars and drove six miles to race start. It amazed me how far that distance seemed that morning. We drove on and on around hairpin turns along cliffs and down into valleys. I thought after I run this first 6.2 miles (10K), I will only have 131.8 miles left to go. I threw that thought out of my head fast. One step at a time. I needed to break down the distance into small sections or lose my sanity.

The official race start was in the middle of nowhere on a random section of road. Everyone was taking more pictures and chattering. I didn't have anything to say. I gave everyone a hug, then Mark, Bill, and I gathered behind the start banner, and without further delay, Rajat started the countdown. Suddenly, two huge Chinese trucks barreled around the corner heading straight for us. We dodged to the side of the road as the trucks whipped by, then returned for the countdown. We were off.

After two weeks waiting around and mentally stressing over the expedition, I was now free to run. All my fear and tension evaporated on that road. Moving through space settled me. The temps were mild and there was no wind. I rounded the first corner and enjoyed perfect peace with my running shoes lightly tapping the road, the crews and caravan behind me. Mark was ahead, the powerful muscles of his legs taking big strides. Bill was behind me, which was unusual, but I knew he liked to start slow, and it would only be a matter of time before he passed me. And so I ran.

I started struggling early. From race start at 14,000 feet, we had to run 26 miles straight up to the top of Khardung La at 18,000 feet. Psychologically, I knew that if I made it over the first peak, it would be a huge accomplishment and give me confidence to pull through the rest of the race. If I made it. I power-walked as the rutted road began to get very steep. I took deep breaths and pictured the oxygen entering my lungs and traveling to my muscles.

I didn't dare look up. The peak was so far away and I was gasping for air. I had to concentrate on the road directly in front of me. My mantra was: Move through Space. Breathe and Move. You are

Commitment Ceremony at 18,000 ft., Khardung La

strong, you are tough. Move through Space. I called on the strength of my sisters: Kathy, Karen, Eileen, Colleen, and Bridget. I called on women power and thought of the strong women in my life, my daughters Bailey and Taylor, my mom Mary Jane, my girlfriends, Jane, Nancy, Tish, Anne, Michelle, Ellen. I conjured up all the strength I could muster in order to keep moving.

After a while Bill caught up to me and we held hands by the side of the road. Bill and I had a secret goal at the top of Khardung La. We wanted to reach the top together so that we could have a private commitment ceremony. It was an idea we had formed before we came to Leh. The depth of our relationship was growing. A commitment ceremony, where we expressed our love on the top of the world, was a romantic idea that appealed to both of us.

We didn't share our plans with anyone but a few of our crew members. Earlier in the week I had a prayer flag blessed by the Lama, and Bill and I placed it strategically near the spot where we wanted our ceremony. The Lama told me to write all the names of our family and friends on the flag and place it on Khardung La for good luck. Our designated commitment spot was an outcrop overlooking the entire city of Leh, high up in the clouds.

Bill and I also purchased two silk pashmina scarves and two rings for the ceremony. We bought the sapphire rings near the Taj Mahal and had Sindhu hold both the rings and scarves for us until we reached the top.

Needless to say, I wanted to keep up with Bill! Not only for our ceremony but also because I didn't want him waiting at 18,000 feet any longer than necessary.

I was wondering if the commitment idea was a good one, when I started to feel nauseous halfway up the mountain. I started feeling weak, but I couldn't eat. When the trucks drove past, the exhaust fumes made me feel worse. I turned my head and covered my mouth to try to avoid it. I slowed down. I had stopped and sat on a rock by the side of the road to gather energy.

Bill ran by and asked how I was doing. Then he said, "I hate to tell you this, but there is a hand grenade right behind you." I didn't understand what he had said. I looked from his face and followed his eyes to the place where a dark object lay on the snow. It was an actual hand grenade with the pin in it sitting about two feet from me in the snow.

I jumped up and shrieked, "Oh, my God!" Adrenaline shot through my brain and body. I couldn't help but think, how did it get there? Did a military truck come along and the hand grenade just bounced off the truck? It was mind-boggling. My new motivation, to escape the bomb, propelled me up the road after Bill. I ran straight up, mile after mile, until suddenly I noticed I was grasping for air and my short-lived stamina began to dwindle. I wanted to get to the top. I wanted to meet up with Bill, who now was way ahead and going strong.

As I was reaching the top, I took a second and stopped. The wind was blowing, it was cold, and I looked out over the valley and down below where I had come. I saw the yaks next to the stream and all the jagged formations of snow. It was a beautiful sight. I was trying to take a minute and realize what I was doing and what was happening. This was simply amazing. Lama Tsephel had always told me to be in the moment, not the past or the future. So, I took in the wonderful moment near the top of a peak on the edge of the world. Just as I was in my nirvana moment, I saw through my half-closed lids that Randy was marching over to me. He didn't look happy.

"I don't like what is happening here!" His angry face was red. "There is an avalanche on the other side of the peak, and Rajat has left us all here to rot!" I had already heard from the other crew members that an avalanche covered the road ahead. Mark had run over it because he was afraid the army would stop him if he asked permission. I wasn't worried because I knew it would take me a long time to get over the peak and I was hoping the army would have it cleared by then. Randy was having a meltdown. I was annoyed because I needed all my brainpower to keep moving. I didn't need negative input or angst. I had plenty of my own. He kept yelling and complaining, and I felt like throwing him off the cliff there and then. Tension was high. I realized my visions of pushing him over the edge were my own negative energy and misery. I wanted to lash out because I was so uncomfortable, so miserable that all I could think about was getting inside the crew van and lying down to sleep. I put my hand on Randy's shoulder to calm him.

"Randy," I said. "This is ultramarathon running. This is what we do. You need to calm down." That did not soothe him. He stomped towards the car as Sindhu came over. I asked her to keep Randy away from me. I told her I needed to concentrate and he was becoming a distraction. One foot in front of the other . . . one foot. I had crewed for many years so I understood the difficulty of the job. Sometimes I think crewing is harder than actually running the race. I crewed Catherine Todd, a talented, young ultrarunner at Badwater, thirty-seven hours nonstop through Death Valley. She had never attempted the Badwater Ultramarathon before, and she asked me to be on her crew because I had finished and I had experience. I remember when she freaked out and threw up her guts on one of the toughest parts of the course, in 115 degree heat. "I have never thrown up in a race!" she cried after she heaved on the side of the road. She sobbed louder in-between giant wretches. "Oh wow, never puked?! You are in good hands!" I explained. "I'm the queen of barf!" I patted her on the head and got her back on the road. Sometimes people just need a little encouragement. The mind keeps telling you that you can't make it, but others can help turn that around. Sometimes runners need to fool themselves into believing that the pain will go away. We have to rise above the uncomfortable moments of blisters popping in our shoes and barf episodes. Runners often go full circle where we feel well and the blisters aren't so bad, then we dip back into hell with hallucinations and surreal moments of pure agony. Sometimes my stomach knots into a spasm and I can't eat or drink. That's always the worst. If I don't get down the fuel, I'll grow weak and stop. Get something down or fail.

As I approached the top, Sindhu yelled out the window of the crew vehicle that Bill was waiting for me. She was holding the two Indian silk ceremonial scarves—a blue one for Bill and a red one for me—to have something sacred that had been blessed by the Lama to make our commitment ceremony more meaningful.

I saw Bill waiting for me, grabbed the scarves from Sindhu, and ran over to clasp his hands on our little outcropping at the peak. The spot looked out over the mountains and the snowy valley. We both took turns pledging our commitment and love to each other as we exchanged our sapphire rings.

"I love you, Buddy!" I hugged and kissed him and started sobbing with pure joy.

"You are my Molly, my adventure woman," he whispered.

It was a powerful moment on the edge of the world, one of the most memorable moments of my life. The crew kept a respectful distance so we could have a few minutes of privacy. At the conclusion we turned towards Sindhu, Rajesh, and Randy, who were standing nearby ready to continue the race. They all had smiles on their faces, including Randy, who seemed to have calmed down. Meanwhile, Nischal and Sabine, part of Bill's crew, started to show signs of altitude sickness, as they had stayed too long at the top of Khardung La.

Bill gave me a big kiss and hug. "I'll see you at the finish line," he yelled, and off he ran down the mountain. Little did we realize that neither of us would finish.

CHAPTER 17

Crewing at 18,000 Feet

"After she runs the first 25 miles I will know what
kind of day she is having."
—Bailey Sheridan commenting on crewing her mom

I LOOKED DOWN at my sapphire ring and took in the moment as I watched Bill run into the distance. I glanced at the prayer flags that were waving in the wind across from my perch. Bill and I had attached our flag to the sacred area at the top of the mountain. It was waving securely in the breeze.

My crew and I were so excited to be over the top. No one wanted to stay at altitude any longer than necessary. Sindhu handed me my water bottle and joined the rest of the crew in the vehicle and headed down. I began the long descent fourteen miles straight down.

Looking back, my crew thought the toughest part was behind us. It had taken eight long and grueling hours to climb 26 miles to the top of Khardung La. The crew headed downhill so quickly that I realized I didn't instruct them on when to meet me. Glancing at my water bottle, I knew I needed more water and food about three miles ahead. Concerned, I began to run.

The road was gutted and narrow with few areas that a car could safely pull over. The snow was melting from the afternoon sun and large rivers of water were flowing across the road. There was no way around the water, so my shoes were soon drenched. I was anxious to descent into warmer temperatures. I passed a small shrine that was cut out into the mountain. Inside were little statues of the Buddha and a box with rupees spilling out. A long stand of rope held three bells that were tied together. I stopped and rang the bells like I had seen so many truck drivers do. I assumed they were asking for safe passage, and the small shrine was a revered place to make a donation and worship Buddha. So I rang and rang the bells as they echoed loudly off the mountains. '

Three miles down, no crew and my water bottle was empty. I crested a hill and peeked over the edge at the road below. I could not see my crew vehicle anywhere. I suddenly had the sinking feeling that they went all the way to the bottom, the military checkpoint and our check-in station, called South Pullu. I was horrified at the thought that I would not have support for the next 11 miles. I began to feel sick and dehydrated. I imagined the crew assumed since it was downhill I would run to the bottom in no time and meet them. The problem was my depletion from the climb. My stomach was in knots and the ascent had taken most of my reserve. I desperately needed hydration and calories.

Nausea and a killer headache set in. I was still at over 15,000 feet and making slow progress. I ran a few steps then walked and tried to make progress, but my stomach was rolling with internal pain. Mark and Bill were way ahead and the crew vans were gone. I lay on the side of the road in the dirt and put my feet on a rock in an attempt to get rid of my screaming headache. Instead of relief, I started dry heaving, which intensified the pain in my head. I was hoping that the van would come back, but they didn't. No one was there to help. So I had to keep moving. The next few hours were horrible. I found myself angry with my crew for abandoning me. I knew that probably wasn't fair because they had no idea I would take so long to get down the mountain. But the time was passing. Weren't they concerned at the amount of time I had been out of their sight? None of my crew had crewed an ultramarathon and lack of experience was evident. By the time I got to South Pullu, I was in bad shape. I was shaking, nauseated, and dehydrated. I hadn't had anything to eat or drink for hours. I saw the crew vehicle ahead and the crew watching anxiously as I rounded the corner and entered their line of sight. At that moment I saw Rajat's crew car drive up to my crew vehicle. Rajat jumped out, said a few words to my crew, which I could not hear, and then ran up to me.

He said, "Molly, how long have you been without water?"

I mumbled, "Hours."

"You don't look good," Rajat observed. Examining my eyes, he said, "You need to go to the Leh hospital. You are really dehydrated."

I didn't want to go to the hospital and I firmly told him so. I reasoned that I was still coherent. I simply wanted to sit and regroup, to eat and drink until I got my strength back. My crew was anxiously staring at me as Rajat and I had our conversation sitting on the tailgate of the car. I had visions of drinking a giant smoothie and eating a large slice of pizza. My appetite was back. I joked around that I would pay someone 50 bucks for a slice of pizza, but no one was in a joking mood. They were worried about me, and everyone was tired. The sun was going down, the cold was setting in, and the wind was blowing a chill our way. After Rajat and I battled back and forth over the hospital idea, I finally gave in. He convinced me that my recovery would be faster with intravenous assistance, which would get me back to the course sooner. He also promised he would get me a pizza in town, which was the deciding factor.

In most races, if a runner gets an IV, he is disqualified. Rajat assured me that I could continue the race. In a way, it really wasn't a race anymore. Since the venture had never before been attempted and there were so many unknown factors, from the logistics, the weather, and the unstable military conditions, Rajat had to constantly roll with the punches. He had three people, now on different parts of the course, all with crew, and he had to keep them all safe. I imagine it was like climbing Everest for the first time not knowing how bad it could get and not knowing what major obstacles might pop up when least expected.

Rajat marked the spot where I stopped at South Pullu. He pounded a stake in the ground where I would begin when I returned from the hospital. He told me I had plenty of time left to complete the entire distance in the allotted time. So I reluctantly climbed into the support vehicle and we drove to the Leh hospital.

The hospital was filthy. It was similar to a little barn. I expected to see chickens running down the hallway. The beds were streaked with dirt and grime. The entire "hospital" was only one room with a bunch of dirty beds filled with sick people. Patients were lying next to me coughing up phlegm. I envisioned disease and contagion everywhere. A woman with an off-white uniform led me over to a bed. I was still in my running clothes, and as I sat on the bed to swing my feet up, she proceeded to yell at me in Hindi, pointing to my shoes. I hadn't bothered to take off my shoes because the bed covers were so stained. I was amazed that she cared if my shoes where still on in a bed that looked as though it hadn't been cleaned in the last ten years.

The nurse rolled over the IV pole, grabbed my arm, and started to stick me with a needle. I said, "Rajat, is this sanitary?" I had visions of getting some sort of Third World plague.

He assured me that these were indeed doctors and nurses, although I noticed he quietly stepped in after watching the nurse and decided to start my IV himself. Sindhu and Rajesh were at my bedside. Randy had left the room after freaking out at the conditions.

I felt like the whole expedition was too much for him. Yes, the conditions were awful. Yes, it was difficult and unpredictable. But what did he expect when he signed on? (Like Private Benjamin who asked if army clothes come in a color other than green, I expected Randy to ask if there was a place nearby that was flat and warm . . . with lots of oxygen.)

Crewing is a tough job. During the standard 26-mile marathon, which generally takes two to six hours, runners can carry what they need. Besides, such races occur in populated areas, where there are numerous aid stations along with spectators handing out drinks and food. Ultramarathons, on the other hand, can involve elapsed times of twenty-four to sixty hours. Like the pit crew at a NASCAR event, a crew makes or breaks the runner. I had seen crews at Badwater completely break down under the pressure of working together in extreme conditions. If a runner loses her crew to fatigue, fighting, or numerous other issues, she's out of the race. The crew needs to be the foundation of safety and sanity when an emotional and physically drained runner starts to unravel after hours and hours of physical exertion. I knew before we left the U.S. that Randy did not have any idea what crewing involved. He had a romantic concept of being in India on a wild adventure in a fairy tale story of golden temples and exotic locations. All that may be true, but the reality would also involve being stuck in a van with five people for days. No showers, little sleep, and working your ass off to try to keep the runner (me) moving. Randy persistently called me and virtually insisted that he be included on my crew. He decided that he was going to India anyway. He wanted to write about the expedition and take pictures and obviously had his own agenda. I told him he was welcome to come as long as I was not responsible for him. I introduced him to Rajat and let it go at that. Then he showed up in Leh and was assigned to be on my crew. Big mistake.

I was angry at myself for allowing Randy on my crew, and I was even madder at him for not dropping out once it got tough. It was as if he wanted to stay and complain about everything. The cards were dealt. DEAL WITH IT! It was a monumental task to focus on the task at hand with Randy constantly whining and complaining. He was on my nerves and creeping under my skin.

As I lay in the hospital bed, I wondered if Randy would continue after I got my IV. Then Bill popped his head around the corner. He had also staked out on the course when he heard I was in the hospital. I was horrified, and I told everyone to get him out of there! With his raspy voice and cold, I knew he would catch something awful in the barn hospital with the cracked plaster walls and coughing patients. We ended up quickly waving to each other as his crew whisked him away.

Rajat then told me Bill had gotten sick on the course and thought he was going to collapse. He was on his way to a guesthouse to lie down to see if he could recover and continue. We seemed to be crashing and burning.

While I was lying there with my IV chatting to Rajesh and Sindhu, a local man came into the room, held up on either side by his family members, causing a huge commotion. He was coughing and throwing up and in extreme agony. The nurses were trying to help him lie down, but he started flailing his arms and gasping for breath. There were no curtains to divide the patients, so everyone watched as one nurse put a bowl under him to catch his retching while others tried to get him to lay down. I tried to avert my eyes in order to give him some sort of privacy, but there was so much upheaval that I couldn't help but watch in horror. Rajat stood next to me, trying to block me from the scene. He was making nervous glances at the sick man, who was now in the bed next to me, making gurgling sounds like his lungs were full of fluid. He was clearly struggling to get every breath and everyone seemed helpless. I briefly saw the man's friend or brother, I never knew which, reach out and hold his hands while words were exchanged. The man in distress was struggling to say something in Hindi. Suddenly, silence. All struggling and sound stopped in the bed next to me. We all exchanged looks. He had just died.

Rajat turned to me and said, "Molly, I think we should go now." I noticed my IV wasn't done, but Rajat yanked the needle out of my arm and escorted me out of the eerily quiet room.

I found out later that the man died of altitude sickness. I don't know where he came from or how long he was at high altitude. I don't know his story, but he died there in the bed next to me in Leh. Weeks later, Rajesh told me that the dying man had grasped his friend's hand and told him in Hindi that he knew he was dying. Rajesh heard all the words that were exchanged, the man's heartfelt good-byes to his family, and was deeply shaken by the scene as we all were. When I left the hospital, I convinced myself that he wasn't dead. I didn't want to know and I didn't ask anyone around me. I just pretended that they gave him a shot and put him to sleep. Deep down, however, I knew he had died. I could tell from the feeling in the room, from the look of shock on the faces around me. I couldn't face the idea that someone right next to me had just died of altitude sickness, especially since I had more altitude to conquer, including another 18,000-foot peak.

After the hospital turmoil, Rajat took Sindhu and me to a small guesthouse to lie down and rest before I went back out on the course. He also gave us huge slices of pizza. I never knew how Rajat always had the resources to come up with equipment, food, whatever, in the most dire situations. How can you get a pizza in the middle of the night in Leh, India?

I lay down in the little bed at the guesthouse trying to gear myself up for getting back out on the course. I locked away the hospital experience in the back of my mind. I put to rest the anxiety of the whole ordeal and settled in to get what rest I could and tackle the mountain again in a short time. Before the light went out, I was admiring my beautiful commitment ring that Bill had given me up on Khardung La. It seemed like years ago. Two hours later, I was back on the course.

CHAPTER 18

Spiders

"It's only when it comes to crunch time that people's true character comes out."
—Virginia Wade

AFTER A COUPLE of hours, Rajat pounded on our door and I got shakily to my feet. The more I moved around, pulling on my warm running tights and blue windbreaker, the better I felt. The rest of the crew members were assembling at the van. Everyone was quiet. At 4:00 a.m., it was still dark outside as we made our way back to the stake at South Pullu. I stepped out of the van and gazed down at my hand to once again admire my ring . . . this time in the cold moonlight . . . but the stone was missing! A big gaping hole stared back at me like a one-eyed Cyclops. No one understood my incoherent yelling as I pulled bags out of the back and scrambled in the dirt searching for my small stone. The thought of beginning my run without my ring was too much to bear. Losing the stone was a bad omen. Everyone was watching me freak out as I tore apart the van. What if something happened and I didn't have that ring? I ran up a frickin' 18,000-foot peak to get that ring! I had to find the stone. Suddenly my hand ran across a lump on the floor. I grabbed the lump, put it up to the interior light, and there was my

163

precious deep blue stone. I clutched it to my chest for a moment, took a deep breath, and put it safely in my pack. Bad omen averted!

The weather turned warm as the sun hit mid-day. I made great time all the way through Leh and stopped briefly at the checkpoint heading out of town. Rajat was there with his team. Rajat said Bill was right behind me and would be catching up soon. Bill had already taken a break the same time as me, so I assumed he got back on the course late.

So off I ran. The next town on our course was Choglamsar, the summer home of the Dalai Lama, whom I had met during the weeks that I had acclimated in Leh. He would walk the streets surrounded by monks while waving to everyone. There was a large gathering one day near the monastery to listen to the Dalai Lama speak. Bill and I sat near him and watched as he spoke to the crowd, throwing his head back and laughing often. He was speaking Ladakhi, but an English translator sat near us. I felt privileged to see His Holiness in person; he seemed to radiate joy and happiness.

My crew drove along at pace with me. Everyone was rested, fed, and in sync with our schedule. I was now in the center of town with bustling traffic and pedestrians. My only problem was the exhaust fumes from the trucks and cars. I kept pulling up my scarf to cover my nose and mouth to cut down the fumes. I caused a stir running through intersections in my blue running shorts and white top. It was hot and I didn't care if the townspeople thought I was a slut running through their streets half naked. Some people stared but others waved and smiled and called out greetings. People were yelling, "Jullay," which means hello. That was the best part of the race for me. I was excited to be there. I kept waiting for Bill to pass, which I knew was inevitable because he is so much stronger. I kept looking behind for Bill's van, but there was no sign of them. I put on my iPod and thought about Bailey, who had loaded it with songs. Her selections were hilarious and interesting, but I could not name a single tune. I got into the zone, into my groove, and was able to make great progress through the little towns up to Karu. I felt inspired and fortunate to be making up time after the cursed IV. On to Upshi. The landscape was desert next to the Sindhu River and the temps were screaming hot, well over 100 degrees. I threw on white pants to protect my legs from sunburn. The traffic was way behind us, and now it was just the hot wind and silence of the desert. I began to feel exhausted. Again the roller coaster. After we entered another little village, I lay down on a little cot at a tea stall and ate some noodles. A woman from the village seemed concerned and offered me her hut. She seemed excited to host me and offered tea. I held up my fresh clothes in an attempt to explain that I wanted to change. She smiled and closed the door to give me privacy. I changed into fresh clothes, shoes, and socks, which immediately lifted my mood. I stepped out of the hut and looked down the miles of road that we had just traveled. No sign of Bill or his crew.

It shouldn't have taken Bill all day to catch me. The creeping suspicion that something had happened to Bill began to take hold in my mind. I kept pushing the thought away; it had no place in my struggle to keep moving. I had to keep myself strong mentally and physically. Bill and I had run a lot of races together. We run as competitors and do not worry about one another. Each of us can stand alone and do what is necessary to get to the finish line. But in this particular race, in such extreme conditions, Bill did not start in top form. His cough and weakened condition at race start weighed on my mind. I looked around at the remote area surrounding me and thought about how fragile our safety was in these tiny towns where medical care was scarce. The overwhelming concern that my partner was out there and not accounted for left me with deep misgiving. It was not like Bill. According to my calculations, he should have easily passed me hours ago. The next major aid station and camp had tents, an outdoor kitchen set up with hot food and staff. I focused all my attention on getting there in the hopes that Bill would arrive at the same time. I had not heard from Rajat or his team all day, and I didn't know how far ahead Mark was, either.

The landscape changed from desert with arid heat and wide-open space to deep canyons on both sides. Dusk had settled and Rajesh was pacing me on a broken dirt road that fell away into a cascading river. The moon rose as we passed little dark huts along the empty road. As the moonbeam hit the river, the water turned iridescent white.

"The river looks like flowing milk!" Rajesh said, as we both stopped and gazed into the flowing liquid. It was indeed foaming milk, frothing its way past us, rolling through the canyon. The crew vehicle backlights were blinking off and on in the distance as the drivers tried to maneuver the vehicle through the cracks and crevices of the broken road. Big chips of asphalt had crumbed into the river where the water seemed to reach up and pull it from the surface. My muscles were sore and a heavy weariness took hold of me. I desperately wanted to stop but forced each step, concentrating on moving towards the small beam of my headlamp. With the moon so bright, the headlamp was not necessary, but I was too tired to remove it. Every time I stopped, it took double the energy to start moving again. I plodded along no longer running, but walking at a gradual climb towards Upshi. Tang Lang La at 18,000 feet lay ahead, but first the camp. All my mental strength was focused on getting to camp to regroup.

I was terrified of the wild dogs near Leh.

Suddenly I heard a low growl to my right. Rajesh swung his right arm in front of me to stop my progress. The growl turned into fierce barking. I saw the outline of two big black dogs, their white teeth snarling in our direction. Rajesh picked up a rock and told me to be still. I glanced ahead and noticed that the crew van was a tiny dot of light in the distance, too far to help.

'Molly, I want you to slowly start walking towards the van.' Rajesh was calm as he picked up more rocks.

The barking was incessant. One of the dogs charged. Rajesh threw a rock and the dog backed down. I moved my stiff leg muscles as quickly as I could, adrenaline now coursing through my body, in an effort to get closer to the crew vehicle. I figured that

I would not have the strength to fight off a dog, so my only hope was to get to the van. Rajesh was moving along with me, holding the rocks and glancing back to check the position of the animals. It wasn't unusual to hear about people in India being attacked by a pack of wild dogs. There are no animal shelters in India and no form of animal control.

We reached the vehicle and the dogs withdrew. Sindhu stepped out and offered me some crackers. My stomach had been upset after the heat of the day, and I hadn't taken in the calories I needed to sustain my energy. Food would help me overcome my extreme fatigue. I tried to force down the crackers, but they tasted dry in my mouth—like trying to swallow dust with a parched throat.

Running a race through the night is both a curse and a blessing. At times the night swallowed up the view so I didn't have to deal with the views of the enormous massive mountains ahead. The concentrated field of vision was only within my headlamp tunnel of light. I could mentally concentrate on the small bright light a few feet ahead of me. For some reason that made me calm, enabling me to zone into my rhythm of movement and feel as if I was making progress. The curse of the dark is that it can seem endless. The view never changes. My headlight would cast ghostly shadows on all sides. Hallucinations played tricks on my mind. Exhaustion and cold, combined with sleep deprivation, can lead to a sort of mental breakdown.

The temperature had dropped, so I stopped to pull on my warmer beanie and gloves. I stopped again and again, annoyed and agitated because I couldn't get warm and my stomach seemed to be in knots, forcing me to gag up the food that hadn't wanted to go down. I lost track of the hours, but I knew I was fumbling my way through the evening. My pace was a shuffle. I had made it over 75 miles, over halfway to the finish, though it felt like a thousand miles in a bad dream which was never going to end.

As Randy paced me, Rajesh and Sindhu sent the car ahead to see how far the aid station was. They returned shortly. The good news was that the camp/aid station was less than 10 miles. My spirits rose. I could get hot food and lie down for a few minutes in order to get my mind refocused on my running. Ten baby miles wasn't bad.

A local Indian guide whom Rajat had hired to run the camp greeted me as we arrived. Our crew vehicle was already parked, and the guide hurried up to me with a warm cup of chai tea and soup. Rajesh, Randy, our driver, and Sindhu all sat around the camp stove and warmed our bodies.

"Mark not far ahead," the Indian man who introduced himself as Vishnu said in broken English. "He here short time ago."

I was surprised that I was so close to Mark at that stage of the race. I had felt like I was going at a snail's pace, but the truth was that I hadn't stopped moving over the course of the day. Randy and Rajesh were looking at me with tired expressions, waiting to see what I wanted to do. I had a total of sixty hours to complete the race. Short rest breaks are allowed as long as you get to the finish line in the time allowed. I had time to spare.

"Let's all climb into the tents and get some rest," I said. "I need to regroup and get out of the cold. Let's rest for forty-five minutes."

I didn't need to say any more. Rajesh and Randy disappeared in two seconds ducking into nearby tents. Sindhu and I got into a tent under a huge tree next to the creek. It was in the middle of the night—maybe 2:00 in the morning. I had my little headlamp on, and I noticed when I was crawling into the tent with Sindhu that there was a spider walking along the floor. I didn't care. I grabbed the spider and just threw it out the flap of the tent. Then I noticed that my light hit another spider at the base of the wall of the tent and again I grabbed it and threw it out the door. I was so very weary. I couldn't wait to lay my head down. I flashed my light over towards my jacket, which I had fashioned into a makeshift pillow. Then I saw a group of spiders scurrying towards me. I became alarmed. As I scooted over to shoo them out, the beam hit the back of the tent where I saw movement. Slowly I raised the beam along the back of the tent . . . slowly . . . up the wall to the roof. The entire tent was alive and moving with spiders—thousands and thousands of spiders. At that moment Sindhu screamed, "Molly! There are spiders on you!"

I shrieked, jumped, and hit my head on the tent pole as I scrambled to get out. My adrenaline hit the roof. I ran from the tent yelling for Vishnu. Sindhu was hitting my clothes, trying to brush off all the spiders that had dropped from the roof onto my body. She was covered with the black creatures as well. Yanking my beanie off my head, I swung and swatted at the mass of insects (okay, arachnids). We both were pelting each other in a wild dance of swinging arms and jerking movements.

The tent had been placed under a tree where every spider in India must have lived. I flashed my light on the tent as I hopped up and down and noticed that the whole exterior was moving. We apparently caused a mass exodus of the spider colony inside.

Vishnu calmly looked over at us as he squatted and warmed his hands in the comfort of the campfire. He slowly stood up as we jumped and screamed and hit the spiders crawling up our bodies.

"Our tent is infested!' I yelled at him. "It is covered in spiders!"

The Indian man calmly walked over and said, "Ah, I fix."

He picked up a towel, went into the tent and began sweeping out the spiders. I was shocked that he had the courage to go in there as it now was even more overrun by thousands of spiders. Full moonlight shimmered on so many black-moving clumps. They were spilling onto the ground from the slanted tent rooftop like a torrential downpour of rain. A black rain of spiders. They teemed onto the grass dispersing in every direction similar to a dark can of paint emptying on a green floor, swirling and rushing in an effort to escape. Sindhu and I looked at each other in disbelief wondering what would become of our camp handyman if he didn't come back out of the tent. What kind of spiders were these anyway? Do they have black widows in India? What about those brown recluse spiders with a vicious bite causing your skin to dissolve to the bone?

Vishnu climbed out of the tent after five minutes. "Okay," he said, "you sleep now," and gestured for us to go back into the tent.

"Oh, no!" I shook my head. "We are not going back in there!" I stared at him as if he were a complete lunatic.

He smiled, "All good." Then he gestured again for us to enter.

"No way." I pointed to another tent rolled up on the ground by the campfire. "We need a new tent. Not here!" I motioned to an area away from the spider infiltration. Vishnu frowned and shrugged, unable to convince us to move back into the Bates Motel. After long minutes of negotiation and hand-waving, as we motioned him to move further and further away from the spider area, he pitched another tent.

We tentatively climbed in but neither of us could sleep. Randy and Rajesh slept through the entire spider attack. All the yelling and shrieking couldn't wake the dead. I envied them. I was wired and felt imaginary spiders crawling up my back and moving down my leg in my new tent.

After I tossed and turned in the tent for a few minutes, I looked over at Sindhu in the dark, her silhouette from the full moon outlined against the canvas. She was as restless as I was.

"Where do you think Bill is?" I asked. "I can't believe that he still has not caught up to us."

I was feeling depressed because Bill was weighing heavily on my mind. I was really exhausted. We were close to the 90-mile mark in the race. Temperatures were dropping again and the cold was creeping into the marrow of my bones. It had been hot, around 100 degrees, during the day and my skin had been burned, which now hurt with the prickling of goose bumps. My muscles ached. I noticed that my right ankle was swollen. Mentally and physically, I was feeling completely overwhelmed and drained.

"Bill will be fine," Sindhu said. "He has a good crew who will take care of him. You should try to get some rest so you can finish this race."

Sindhu's kind words comforted me. I closed my eyes.

CHAPTER 19

Defeat

*"Take into account that great love and great achieve-
ment involve great risk."*
—His Holiness The Dalai Lama

HOURS LATER I jerked awake from a dead sleep. I had dreamed that
I was running and running, unable to stop. I felt disoriented and
deeply exhausted. I jumped up, mad at myself for not setting an
alarm and for taking too much time to rest. The light in the distance
told me that dawn was near. I pressed the light button on my wrist
and 4:00 glowed on my wrist. I had slept for two hours, an hour and
fifteen minutes too long. Thick clouds of frost clung to the freezing
air as I made my way over to the campfire. Vishnu whipped up a
batch of porridge and coffee within minutes. I scanned the area for
signs that Bill's crew had somehow quietly arrived during the night
as we slept, but the other tents were empty and our crew car sat alone
next to the road. A deep quiet surrounded the camp. The big spider
tree and abandoned tent had no sign of creatures this morning. I sat
in the cold morning air trying to get down some porridge as Rajesh,
Sindhu, and Randy began to emerge and gather their belongings. I
knew it was time to start back out on the course. My stomach felt
sick that Bill was not here. I now knew that there was trouble.

Off in the distance I heard the sound of a car. My heart leapt as I pictured the arrival of Bill's crew. Everyone turned to watch a crew vehicle pull into the camp. Rajat jumped out of the car with Shosheild, his driver. He gave me a big hug. With a serious look on his drawn face, he said, "Molly, Bill is very ill. I don't know exactly how he is doing." I took a deep breath. "Yesterday, as he was leaving Leh, Bill got sick and had to go back to the hospital. I have been up with Mark, who has just summited the second peak. There has been no communication with Bill or his crew as we don't have cell service here. There is a small store ahead that opens at 7:00 a.m. We can use their phone and get an update on Bill."

I could tell he was being evasive. "How bad is it?"

Rajat replied, "I don't know. I haven't seen him, and it has been several hours since I have heard anything. They took him back to the hospital. He was having issues." I asked if it was altitude sickness but Rajat didn't know.

Rajat had explained to us earlier that we would be unable to use satellite phones in this area of the course. If the military caught us with a satellite phone, it would mean two years in prison. The Pakistan and China borders were too close. A satellite phone in the hands of a civilian, especially a foreigner, is conclusive evidence of spying.

I tried to hold back the tears. They came anyway as I sat on the tailgate of his car and sobbed. I asked Rajat more questions. When did he last see Bill? How did he look? Was his condition life-threatening? I knew Rajat didn't want me to worry. He didn't want to throw a mental obstacle in my way and interfere with my concentration. I put my hand on Rajat's arm and said, "You need to tell me everything you know."

He said solemnly, "Molly, Bill is not coming back to the race. They will fly him to a hospital in New Delhi."

I let the words sink in. My worst fears. I was completely devastated. I needed to think, think, think. I wrapped my hands around my head. I knew Bill was in good hands with Rajat's team. I felt confident that the team could handle an emergency and Bill would be cared for. But how bad could this get? I didn't know what to do. Should I continue to be a competitor and let race management handle Bill's condition? Or should I drop out and go to Bill? What good could I do him? I was close to the 100-mile mark. Should I finish and then rush to his side? The problem with continuing was that we would be driving back from the finish line in the Morey Plains to New Delhi, a three-day trip by car with no communications. So I would not know anything about Bill's condition for three more days. Meanwhile, I was thinking about my crew. I didn't want to disappoint them. They had come this far. My mind was in turmoil. I began to gather my bags and equipment at camp. I told Rajat that I was going to go back on the course and continue the race. I asked him to please come and let me know about Bill's condition as soon as the shops opened and he received word.

Sindhu, Randy, and I drove back to the place we had staked out a mile down the road. Randy leaned over the back seat and said, "You are making a huge mistake. Bill could die! If I were you, I would give up this race and go to New Delhi. Rajat cannot be trusted!"

During this rant, I put up my hand and said, "Enough!" I got out of the car and asked Sindhu to pace me. The crew vehicle with Randy drove ahead.

"Sindhu, keep Randy away from me." I was shaking I was so mad at him. "I don't want any of Randy's opinions. He is stressing me out. Does he think I don't know how bad this is? Does he think I am an idiot!?" I knew that some of Randy's words were true. I knew that Bill could die of even a small complication here in the Himalayas. I needed to find out if they already had flown Bill to New Delhi. Could Bill possibly have recovered since Rajat last saw him over twenty-four hours ago? Was it possible that he was now stable and the situation had changed for the better? I wasn't ready to abandon the race with lack of information.

"You will make the best decision," Sindhu said as she looked over with her compassionate eyes. "Randy does not mean to annoy you. He is concerned. Listen to your heart. It will all be well." I appreciated her soothing Indian accent and perfect English.

I soon slowed to a walk and then started sobbing. My only thought at the moment was to continue with the race until I received more information. I also needed to breathe and find peace so I could think clearly. Moving through space always settled my mind and gave me clarity.

I prayed to Buddha in this land of his. I prayed to Mary, which I learned to do in my world. I asked both of them for direction. I was an emotional wreck. To stay in the race, I had to pretend that Bill was not seriously ill, but I couldn't block that fact from my mind. Then the thought occurred to me that I might finish the race, only to then be told that Bill had died. How would I feel? The race would mean nothing. The worst-case scenario played out in my mind. I thought about the overwhelming love I had for Bill, my adorable partner and best friend. The reality of the situation slammed into me like a speeding train. I came to the realization that I could never make it over Tang Lang La while worried about Bill's fate. If I didn't have my mental strength, my body could not summon the physical strength. I turned to Sindhu. "The race is over for me."

She said nothing but held my hand as we jogged up to the crew vehicle. I climbed in and told them to drive into town to find Rajat. Randy started to speak, but I held up my hand and commanded silence. We found Rajat on a phone outside of a little store. I jumped out of the car and ran up to him as he was hanging up the receiver.

"Bill is flying out at 10:30 a.m. from Leh to New Delhi. Neetu is with him. He needs to get to a hospital." Worry was etched into Rajat's face.

"Take me to him. Will we make it to Leh before the plane leaves?" I felt sick.

"We have to leave right this minute in order to make it. It's going to take us two hours."

Knowing that Neetu, my faithful friend who had driven me all over Leh on his motorcycle, was with Bill gave me great comfort. I knew he would care for Bill like a member of his own family. I shouted a rushed farewell to my crew as Rajat instructed them to go assist Mark's crew. I hugged each one and thanked them. I jumped in the car with Rajat and leaned out the window and waved and sobbed. We were all crying and waving. It was an awful, abrupt end of a relationship with a faithful crew who hung with me all those hours. Fate dealt her hand. Destiny. I sat in the back of the car as Rajat and Shosheild drove frantically to Leh. Nobody talked. I worked on pulling myself together. I looked out the backseat window at the snowy mountains flying past as we drove at breakneck speeds. We zoomed along all those miles and miles I had painstakingly covered. I was in shock that the race was ending this way. I could not picture big, strong Bill in the hospital. It was a quiet, stressful drive. All I wanted to do was make sure that Bill was okay.

After a tense-filled, whirlwind ride, we finally arrived at the Leh hospital. Instead of going to the room I had been in a day before, we drove to the back of the hospital and the patient rooms. I jumped out of the car and followed Rajat into Bill's room, where Neetu was faithfully standing at the bed. I took one look at Bill and knew he was in danger. He was deathly pale and looked horrible. He had an oxygen mask on in a room and bed that were filthy. The floor was dirt-covered; the walls were cracked with chipped and peeling paint.

Bill opened his eyes slowly and murmured, "Oh, no. You quit the race."

I replied, "Buddy, how are you doing?" I put my hand on his forehead. Then I embraced him as he lay in the bed. I started crying. My heart swelled with love. I was relieved to see him, but I was terrified at how sick he looked.

He said, "I am having terrible stomach pains. I'm pretty much a mess."

I sat down next to him for a few minutes and held his hand. He was trying to sit as Neetu was helping him get clothes on for the flight. Bill told me that Neetu had stayed at his bedside the entire night and took him back and forth to the bathroom. As Neetu ran to put a pack of Bill's things in the car, Bill said, "I owe Neetu my life. I thought I was going to die last night. He never left my side and he slept on the floor in the dirt next to my bed." He stopped and closed his eyes from the exertion of talking.

I could tell as Bill spoke that he was in terrible pain. Looking down, I realized I was still in my running clothes, my shoes were caked with dirt, my hair was plastered to my head, and I was filthy. Finding my way to the bathroom to change into a clean T-shirt and jeans, I held my breath. The bathroom was used by numerous patients and was full of filth. I didn't recognize myself in the mirror. I looked like I was an old bag woman. I tried to clean up, but the bathroom was so disgusting that I didn't even want to put my hands in the water in the sink. I needed to get Bill out of there fast. The longer he stayed there, the greater the chance of disease and infections. I tucked myself into the corner of the room and pulled on the clean clothes, brushed out my hair and put it into braids. That would have to do. As we left for the airport, Rajat reported that Mark was still going strong. I told Rajat to tell Mark that we wished him success and would be waiting to hear the good news of his completion.

I was tired from my run, completing almost 100 miles in the Himalayas, but I had renewed energy flowing from deep within. My mission was to protect Bill. Watching him made me forget about my own aches and injuries.

Rajat took care of everything. He was constantly on the phone calling to make sure the flights were set for Bill and that transportation to the hospital in New Delhi was arranged when we arrived. Bill was in so much pain. No one seemed to know what was the matter with him. I couldn't wait to get him out of the Leh hospital. I didn't even know why they called that place a hospital—it was a barn with a dirt floor. Being outside in a field would have been a better, healthier option.

Looking back, I don't know how we got Bill from the hospital to the airport. It was scary and tense because I thought Bill was going to pass out and collapse, and we wouldn't be able to get him out of Leh to New Delhi. Any place was better than Leh. There was no help there. Even though I love the city of Leh and consider it a jewel in the center of the stunning Himalayan Mountains, it's not a place anyone wants to be with a medical emergency.

Every muscle in my body was tense, compounded by a major stress headache, as we ushered Bill through the airport. Rajat and Neetu had guided us through the airport up to security, but looked on helplessly on as we struggled. At the same time as I was maneuvering all 6-foot-3-inches of Bill, his entire weight bearing down on my shoulders, I was grabbing all our gear, suitcases, equipment, and flinging them through security. Bill could hardly stand, and the security police looked at him suspiciously. Two security guards came up to Bill and spoke insistently in Hindi. I looked back at Rajat, who bounded past the guardrail urgently pushing to help us. More security guards rushed our way as Rajat spoke rapidly in Hindi, explaining the situation.

After buckling Bill into his seat, I tried not to think about how bad this situation could get. Bill was physically fragile and in danger. He rarely spoke and mostly he kept his eyes closed. Sweat poured off his body. His skin was burning hot, and he seemed to grow worse by the minute.

I looked out the window as the plane lifted off the ground, taking us away from the green fields of Leh nestled in the massive mountains. We lifted away from our dreams, away from accomplishing our goal of finishing the race. A selfish feeling of failure washed over me. I would not be the first woman to finish the race. Bill would not be the first American man who finished.

I remembered a visit to one of the nearby monasteries. I sat with one of the monks and we got into a conversation about destiny. He held my hand and told me, "Our life is 50 percent our own decisions and 50 percent destiny. We must find out how to live with the 50 percent that is our destiny."

Our destiny was to not finish the race. I sadly looked down on the country that I had grown to love. The mountain mist closed in as we rose higher into the air. I whispered my good-byes to Leh. The clouds closed and she was gone.

When we arrived in New Delhi, Vijay picked us up and drove straight to the hospital. It was as clean and as efficient as any U.S. hospital. I was thrilled that they got Bill right into a private room with a sofa bed for me. The doctors immediately convened, performed tests, and blasted his body with antibiotics. When Bill was settled, I ran down and grabbed a bite to eat at the hospital food court. When I returned to the room, there at the foot of Bill's bed was adorable Pramond, my bodyguard who had been airlifted back to New Delhi for altitude sickness. He was leaning over Bill, who was sleeping.

Pramond looked over at me with a half-smile on his face. "I was your bodyguard, now I am Bill's." He stood at the foot of Bill's bed like a sentinel, that entire day and into the night.

The Indian doctor told me Bill had a gangrene gall bladder and needed surgery. The procedure was going to take place in the States, but it took all week to stabilize Bill. Through the next several days the room was filled with doctors. At first I thought it was because of his serious condition. Then I found out that Bill was considered a celebrity. The hospital staff found out that the patient in room 207 was Dr. William H. Andrews, one of the top biologists in the world. The doctors wanted to meet him. They came in and asked him questions on telomere biology. They sat by his bed. They took pictures with Bill propped up on pillows! They all left their cards and wanted to stay in contact with Bill.

Bill's personal doctor from the U.S. called Bill repeatedly and conferred with the Indian doctors. They all agreed that the gall bladder attack was not related to the run. It was just bad timing.

During the third night in the hospital as Bill was being pumped full of antibiotics, word came to us that Mark Cockbain had successfully completed the race. We celebrated with apple juice. Mark and Rajat showed up not long after. Mark shared his story about hallucinating in the freezing snow at the top of Tang Lang La and suffering hypothermia. After Bill and I had flown to New Delhi, our crews joined forces with Mark's crew to help get him to the finish. We all sat together in Bill's hospital room sharing our varied stories, putting the missing pieces together.

Bill turned to us and said, "Whoever doesn't end up in the hospital wins this race."

Everyone laughed. Mark was the only one who missed the accommodation of the Leh hospital. Mark pulled out his trophy that Rajat had given him and shared his victory. He was getting ready to fly back to London. We all hugged and wished each other a safe journey home. It was bittersweet to see Mark leave, as Bill wasn't stable enough to make the trip home yet.

I was so proud of Mark. Bill and I stayed up for hours late into the night after Mark left talking about our joy that he had accomplished what so many had said was impossible. We talked about fate and destiny. The adventure led us to India, but our destiny in 2010 was to not complete the race.

The interesting thing about adventure is that it is inherently unpredictable. It also comes with a certain amount of risk. The risk to continue the race when Bill was in the hospital was too much of a price to pay.

I was sitting in Rajat's guesthouse gazing out the window at a black, angry sky. After seven days, our flight to the States was in the morning and I was ready to go home. I had no regrets. There was a monsoon in full force outside—tons of rain, crashing thunder and lightning. It was as if the final curtain had drawn and closed on this adventure. I certainly fell in love with the people. They were sincere, warm, and helpful beyond common courtesies. I freed myself of expectations and freed myself from what others wanted or needed me to be. I did my best.

I stared into those dark clouds and remembered my first view of Leh, so many weeks before. A lifetime ago. Up in the plane on the first trip to Leh, the clouds had parted as I gazed out on her fertile green valley and massive snow-covered peaks, love at first sight. How ironic that on the return flight home from Leh, Khardung La hid behind her veil. The clouds closed in as if I had become blind, the journey was over and Shangri-La hidden. I knew standing there in Rajat's home in New Delhi, my last night in India, gazing at the thick bolts of lightning that flashed in the distance, that my destiny was not over. I had to go back to the Himalayas.

Chapter 20

Redemption—My Second Attempt

"Let's Party!"

**—Doc John Vigil, in a raging snowstorm
at 18,000 ft., Tang Lang La**

INDIA CHANGED MY life in a profound way. For months after my first trip, my head and heart were floating somewhere at 18,000 feet, resting on the soft snow of Khardung La. Each and every day for a full year I thought about the race in the Himalayas, La Ultra The High. I had a single focus of going back in 2011 and finishing the 138-mile distance.

Meanwhile in the last year, I had become a certified coach. I had a deep desire to not only help myself become a better runner but to reach out to others, especially women, to help them discover the benefits of moving through space, which led to starting a company in 2009—Desert Sky Adventures. My company mission statement is "fitness for health and adventure." I created events that inspired people to get up and move. It was fulfilling work, especially helping women who had not taken any time for themselves to exercise or even walk. I identified with all of them.

I had also spent that year planning my race in the Himalayas. I asked Bailey, who had been my crew chief at Badwater, to accompany me. No one knew me better than Bailey. She was wise beyond her twenty years. She had wanted to travel to India the first year, but

I was concerned that I couldn't concentrate on my race if I was worried about her safety. After witnessing Rajat and his team in action the first year, I had full confidence that the adventure would be safe. I also invited my other Badwater crew member, Dr. John Vigil, "The Stretch Doc." John is a chiropractor and fascial stretch therapist. Not only is he a dear friend, we are also training partners. John is an excellent endurance athlete. His personality was well suited to difficult situations both as an athlete and as crew. Just like Bailey, he is calm and collected. Both Bailey and John had been tested in the toughest crewing conditions at Badwater. Their presence gave me incredible confidence.

I changed my meal plan for my second attempt. The spicy Indian food had upset my stomach the first year. I had lost weight and consequently suffered for it during the race. Bill had researched the Isagenix company and told me about the purity of the products. So, I was packing a suitcase full of their protein shakes, energy bars and supplements. I wanted to be self-sufficient in India and not depend on local food.

Arriving in India, July 2011, John, Bailey, and I met the runners and their crews. There were six other runners at the event: Lisa Tamati, my ultrarunning friend from New Zealand; Jason Rita, Samantha Gash, and Cath Todd, all Australians; Sharon Gator from Great Britain; and my good friend Ray Sanchez, a talented American runner, whom I ran with in New Zealand.

Ray Sanchez made me laugh every minute of every day. He kept calling me the VO5 girl (from the old commercial about twenty years ago). In the middle of the market he would yell across the street, "There's the VO5 girl. She's famous!" And all the townspeople would look over and think we were crazy. I started calling him Famous Ray. He was always the life of the party.

We got settled into the acclimation period, sightseeing during the long days and going up to Khardung La every other day to condition our bodies. I kept visiting the monastery in search of Lama

Tsephel. The other monks told me that the Lama was visiting His Holiness the Dalai Lama and he might not return before my race start. I kept checking every day anyway. They explained that the monastery where Lama Tsephel was staying was only accessible by foot, a three-day walk through the mountains. The Lama had sent me a letter inviting me to the monastery, but I didn't have enough time (or energy reserve) to walk there and back before the race.

Barry Walton, a videographer, was filming the race this year. He was interviewing everyone and asking me about the obstacles and difficulties we faced during the first attempt. Lisa and Sam, the two other women runners, were also asking my opinion about what to expect during the race, and I did my best to instill confidence in them, but I could not conceal the fact that both Bill and I had been hospitalized (not to mention lynch mobs, avalanches, and spiders). Cath Todd struggled with altitude the entire first week of acclimation and was unable to start the race. She was sent home by Rajat. When she departed, it left all of us feeling vulnerable. We all had our own share of people back home telling us we were crazy. Actually, that's been one of the most common reactions when non-runners have learned that I run ultramarathons: "You must be crazy!" they exclaim, but they completely miss the point.

Like mountain climbing or exploring, ultrarunning is an adventure of unimaginable proportions. If not for running, I would never have experienced the sand dunes of the Sahara, the fog-enshrouded mountains of New Zealand, or the lamas and their Buddhist temples. More than that is the exhilaration of spirit that results from attempting something extraordinary—something that requires extreme physical effort and unimaginable mental fortitude. Imagine how Sir Edmund Hillary felt when he stood atop Mr. Everest in 1953. Or how Randy Bannister felt when he was the first human to run a mile in under four minutes. They were not crazy for attempting those feats, and neither are ultrarunners.

Nakamura at Shanti Stupa, Leh

Early one morning, I asked Bailey and John if they would like to go up to the Shanti Stupa Temple that stood on a hill in the middle of Leh. There are 557 steps that lead up to the white structure, hand-painted with deities and Buddha. Inside the Stupa are ancient scrolls and the teachings of Buddha. We bundled up before the crack of dawn and made our way along the quiet, dark streets of Leh, our pilgrimage to the temple.

The red-robed monks were already chanting when we slipped our shoes off and joined them. There were several foreigners in the group this morning sitting cross-legged at the foot of Buddha. Then a monk with a golden robe entered. He sat down in front of us and eyed a tourist behind me who had a guitar at his side. The chanting stopped and the monk with the golden robe asked in English, "Can you play us a song?" In response the man sang a beautiful song in French while strumming the guitar.

After he was done, the monk asked, "May I play a song for you?" He ducked behind a curtain and came back with his own beautiful guitar. Then he sat down and began to play classical guitar. The music was so lovely that all of us in the room began to look over at each other in awe, wondering if we were dreaming. The music brought tears to my eyes. When finished, he began to sing and play "Imagine" by John Lennon. He played several more songs as we were all swept away in an otherworldly moment.

When he stopped playing, the other people got up, thanked the monk, and made their way to the door. Bailey, John, and I continued to sit. I was mesmerized. The monk asked, "Would you like to see my other guitars?" We all nodded our heads. He got up and gestured for us to follow. We went behind the curtains to his private area. He had a half dozen guitars, picked one out, and began playing the blues. When he stopped playing, he told us that his name was Nakamura and asked if we were tourists in Leh.

I told him that I was running a race through the Himalayas and Bailey and John were crewing me. I explained the race as he listened intently. On a whim I said, "Would you please bless us?"

He looked at me with his soft brown eyes, "You don't need a blessing. You are already blessed by the moon, the earth, and the stars. Life is 50 percent choices and 50 percent destiny. You have made your choice and now you must go to your destiny."

"Well," I answered, "can you bless us anyway?"

He laughed. "The toughest challenge for human beings is to accept their destiny. If, in a previous life, you stole from people, in this life, someone will probably steal from you. That is Karma. It is dealing with destiny that people find difficult." He stared at me. "You have already made your choice, now it is your destiny."

I actually felt peaceful about the monk's comments. At that point heaven and earth could not have stopped me from running that race.

I had made the choice. I didn't know what my destiny was, but I was about to find out.

We wandered over to the outside of the temple and the beautiful Shanti Stupa tower. The plaque at its base was dedicated to the founder of Shanti Stupa, Gyomyo Nakamura, a Japanese monk dedicated to world peace. It turned out that our guitar-playing monk was the founder and leader of the temple. I wished I had asked him if he was a runner. I had read about the Marathon Monks of Mount Hiei in Japan. They travel 52 miles every day in their quest for enlightenment. They believe that running elevates the mind and is a pure form of meditation. The marathon monks are similar to the Lung-gom-pa runners of old Tibet, who are a legend in the Himalayas. They appear to fly as they run, floating above the ground as if in a trance. There are reports that the monks could travel non-stop for forty-eight hours while covering more than 200 miles.

The day arrived and we began the caravan of cars over the mountain to race start outside Khardung Village. This time, to avoid further riots, we used the union workers and their cabs for the entire race. When we passed through the border check, there were no angry men attacking our vehicles. No one was trying to pull me out of the car or punch my pacer.

The night before the race I lay down on the floor in my sweats and visualized the race. I was picturing running up Khardung La once again as well as the other parts of the course I knew in my mind. I refused, however, to go on a team trip to Tang Lang La for a review of that part of the course. I did not want to see Tang Lang La until I was in the race and summiting its 18,000-foot peak, the spot where I had to abandon the race the year before. I wanted to take it on when I was actually on the course facing the challenge. Focusing on Khardung La was tough enough. I heard that Tang Lang La was the mother of all mountains . . . huge switchbacks with more snow and difficult gutted roads. It was too much to think about.

Bailey was rolled up next to me on a mat on the floor. I thought she was sleeping but she knew what I was thinking. "Mom, I have your back tomorrow. You are going to do awesome out there."

"Thanks, Bay Bay," I answered. I was filled with love for my daughter and thankful she was there. "I will do my best. Remember to be safe and stay with John and . . ."

"Mom," Bailey interrupted patiently, "Remember our rule?"

"Oh, yeah, right," I replied. "Sorry."

Our rule was a pact we had made five years before when we ran a 26-mile marathon together. She was fifteen. We got into a big argument in the middle of the race. "Mom!" she yelled as we were halfway through the event. "Stop being a mother! Treat me like a competitor! I am trying to run my race!" She had stopped me in my tracks. I realized I was mothering. After the race, we made a pact that when we were competing we were not mother/daughter but fellow competitors.

It was good for me to let go of all my kids. They had grown into adults now. My mothering ways were now relegated to giving advice when asked. I had loved those days of having them all home and watching their every move. I loved every minute of being a mom, the ultimate adventure. I felt like I did a pretty good job raising them. Now I needed to support them as needed. It was no longer a 24/7 job. And at times, they supported me.

I rested my head on my mat. I knew I had little sleep ahead of me because nerves would keep me up all night. The race was here. On to destiny.

Start line with my fellow competitors

CHAPTER 21

Getting High

"Out on the road there is fitness and self discovery and the person we are destined to be."
—George Sheehan

THE 2011 ULTRA HIGH was about to start. We had all sent family and friends emails and updates. Taylor and Devin were following every message and update on Facebook. Colleen was keeping my dad and brothers and sisters updated. I looked for emails every chance I could. It was comforting and gave me confidence to know that I had so much support at home. Sometimes the Internet in Leh would bomb out for days on end. We never knew how long we had. Bill, who stayed home to do his science research, had sent about a hundred love notes. I knew how hard it was for him not to be with me experiencing the race again. He gave me incredible words of encouragement, and I missed him terribly.

The gun sounded and the six runners took off. I stayed back, conserving energy, knowing that Khardung La was a long haul straight up for the next 26 miles.

During the ascent, my stomach was queasy and I struggled. The climb was so much more difficult than I'd remembered. The uphill switchbacks went on and on. I was by myself, nearly doubled over wheezing for air. When I finally reached the summit, all of the other runners and crews had disappeared into the distance.

When I reached South Pullu, about 40 miles into the race, I felt like aliens were attacking from within. When I descended into Leh, it was 11:00 p.m. I couldn't continue. I lay down for a few minutes to try to get my stomach settled. Feeling better, I was able to make up time through Karu then on to Upshi, the 100-mile mark.

I missed the medical checkpoints the entire race. By the time I arrived, they had moved on. I was so far behind that everyone pretty much ruled out my chances of success. The medical team was ahead with the rest of the athletes, and it was too difficult for them to cover the entire distance between the first place runner and me. No problem. I had Bailey and John and I didn't need medical attention. My early struggle with my nutrition brought on by high altitude wreaked havoc on my performance and my focus. I just wanted to run. But at times I had to power-walk uphill and drag myself along the rural towns toward enormous Tang Lang La, which lay ahead. I believed I could get through this is if I kept moving and could manage to keep food down.

Bailey and John were steadfast supporters. I also had Jigme Stanzin, a local Ladakhi man, who was our interpreter and Lamchun (our Ladakhi driver). Both tirelessly drove and maneuvered the crew vehicle across the vast barren mountains of India into the remote Morey Plains. They all faithfully supported me for unending hours. It was hot in the valleys, then dropped to freezing at night. The roads at times were nonexistent. I was worried during parts of the race as I watched the crew vehicle drive past me on roads dangerously narrow, with a mountain wall on one side and a 5,000-foot death drop on the other. The roads had been washed out and there was barely room for one vehicle. I often saw the back wheels spinning as vehicles struggled through gutted and muddy roads.

As I approached the assent to Tang Lang La, 113 miles and forty hours into the race, I had been running in freezing rain and sleet for eight hours. A base camp had been set up at Rumste, a remote mountain area at the foot of Tang Lang La, where runners (and crew) could catch a little sleep and eat some warm food before the huge assent to the 18,000-foot summit. The thought of what awaited me at that base camp kept me going as I continued to place one foot ahead of the other in the freezing darkness. About ten miles from camp, I sent my crew ahead to get some rest while John paced me the last few miles.

It was nearing 11:00 p.m. as John and I trudged ahead in the dark and rain. We entered Rumste and searched for signs of the camp. As the town faded behind us, we realized that somehow we had missed the camp, and we were now headed up the mountain. John and I were lost. Faced with no other choice, we dismally retreated back down in the dark, flashing our lights into huts in the small remote village, desperately envisioning hot food and a cot. I wanted so desperately to put my feet up for ten minutes. I was soaked to the skin with cold snow and sleet. I was exhausted beyond measure. We were over an hour beyond where we thought the camp should have been.

Backtracking. Few things are worse in any type of long distance race. Every ounce of energy is precious. As runners, we obsess over ways to build up and conserve our energy. We eat selected foods. We sometimes rest or briefly sleep in order to recoup lost energy. Every mile represents an incremental drain of precious energy. To run the same mile twice, and therefore lose energy without advancing toward the finish line, is beyond disconcerting. Yet here we were—running backwards, away from the finish line. All the while I was thinking that I would later have to run up this road again—covering the same ground for the third time.

In addition, by missing the camp, we had prolonged our struggle in the freezing darkness, and we had delayed the moment when we could consume warm food and lie down on a warm, comfortable cot. Running back toward Rumste, with these thoughts careening through my mind, I couldn't have been more depressed. Tears welled up in my eyes, then promptly froze to my cheeks. But there was nothing we could do except . . . keep running.

When we failed to arrive at camp, Bailey knew something was wrong and grabbed Jigme and started searching for us. They finally found us running around Rumste, freezing cold and soaked to the skin. We put a stake in the road to mark where we would return in a couple of hours. They loaded us into the car and drove us into camp. We were so relieved. In spite of backtracking, in spite of delaying our union with warm food and a bed, we were now saved. Depression turned to joy as we arrived at camp.

During the drive, Bailey and Jigme told us that all of the runners had been in camp for hours. Earlier in the day the decision had been made, due to the snowstorm on the mountain, to send a van up Tang Lang La to pick up the runners and return them to camp. Each had staked out his/her position on the mountain and rode back to camp. Meanwhile, John and I were out in the snow and sleet trying to find the camp. (Later, we discovered we had missed a sign that had blown down in the wind.)

What we encountered at the camp was dead silence. There was no rejoicing at our rescue. Everyone was asleep. And when we looked around, we discovered that there was not a single cot available. Apparently, the race officials had never anticipated that everyone would be sleeping at the same time. So they didn't have enough cots for everyone. Like musical chairs, the music had stopped and we were the last men standing. I was devastated.

But I had not yet reached the depths of my disappointment.

When we approached the food table, we discovered that every single morsel had been consumed. Runners and crew alike had been famished. They needed calories which would transform into energy—not only to run, but to battle the elements. NO FOOD! If I had possessed the energy, I would have screamed.

And no one cared. The four of us stood there like survivors in a lifeboat, wondering who among us would be the first to collapse. We couldn't go to the store. We didn't have the energy to cry. I was precariously close to a complete meltdown.

We convened a quick meeting. The one undeniable fact was that the clock was ticking and we couldn't wait at camp any longer. My only choice was to keep moving. Already too much time had gone by. The camp could not provide us with shelter or food. It was our defining moment in the race. I looked outside at the cold wind and rain, as we made the group decision to go on. Each member of the crew was instrumental in this decision. If any person decided to discontinue, it would have been over for us.

Having made our decision, I changed clothes, and we notified the race officials and medical team that we were going to resume the race. The medical team responded that I couldn't go up Tang Lang La because of the snowstorm; they had pulled everyone off for safety reasons. I told them I was behind and I wanted to go to the snowline and stake out to catch up my time. We waited for a decision, but there was only confusion among tired people. There was no food, nowhere for us to rest, nothing for us in Rumste.

Then John said, "Molly, let's go. These people don't know what they are doing."

Just then the only two runners who were not at camp, Sharon Gaytor and Ray Sanchez, arrived in a crew vehicle. They had both finished the race and were on their way back to Leh. Sharon had come in first. Ray second. I was so proud that the first American man had completed the race, and I had nothing but admiration for the speed of the top runners. Sharon did not look good at all, and I was worried about her condition. The medical team was swarming all over her. Sharon and Ray had summited the peak ahead of the storm and were able to complete the 138 miles. The rest of us had over 25 miles to go and a huge snowstorm to deal with. I spoke to Ray briefly in the cabin, and he was disappointed that he did not come in first. He looked amazing and did not seem to be suffering from any ill effects after running 138 miles. I said a quick good-bye and congratulated Ray and Sharon as we departed to resume running in the cold, wet, dark night.

I will look back on that night for the rest of my life. We left camp at midnight in freezing rain, sleet, and eventually snow while everyone else slept with warm food in their stomachs. The most challenging moment was stepping back out into the sleet and snow. Every cell in my body shrieked to stop and rest . . . to stay in the hut. I looked down at my feet and saw myself take the first step out into the dark of midnight. It was as if I was in slow motion and my mind was unattached to my body.

It took every ounce of mental strength and toughness I possessed to go out and onward . . . to run past midnight for a second night. Cold to my core, exhausted, and filthy. My crew was tired beyond exhaustion. That moment is etched in time. I still feel that cold and immense darkness. I forced my mind to concentrate, to move through space. I enclosed myself into my inner mantra. My mind cloaked my body in a safety net of meditation.

Lamchun actually offered to pace me. He knew Bailey and John were spent. Jigme got behind the wheel. Lamchun could not speak English very well but he understood the goal. He did not have running shoes and he only had a long sleeve shirt and a vest. I had a cheap dollar store poncho that I handed him as it was the only thing

I had to offer. The sleet and snow was starting to come down hard. Lamchun loved that poncho and kept thanking me for hours as we power-walked together up the mountain. It was the toughest part of the whole race for me. I felt like I was summiting Everest. I felt like a zombie dragging one frozen foot then the other. At 4:00 a.m. the other teams drove past us to go to their staked-out positions on the mountain. No one could believe that I was out there. They clapped and cheered out their windows as they drove past. I was jealous that they had all slept for hours with hot food in their stomachs. I was so miserably tired.

That night I was at my lowest. The mountain was endless. Mile after mile of trudging through the snow and bitter cold was overwhelming. At one point Bailey was standing next to the vehicle as John and I approached. There was a strobe light blinking on Bailey's head, and she began to dance . . . a crazy robot dance. John started howling with laughter. At first I just stared, attempting to comprehend what I was seeing. She continued to dance with her jerky robot movements. It was hilarious and I had my first laugh in a long time. The brevity lightened my spirit and eased my stress and anxiety. We all got hysterical, on the side of a mountain, in bitter cold, at 17,000 feet, watching a dancing robot with a strobe light on her head.

After a few minutes of brevity, I sank low again into the depths of stress. I couldn't breathe. The switchback trail of snow, sleet, and mud was endless. Bailey was quiet, bundled and hooded in her jacket. She looked at me with concern and suggested I stop for a few minutes to try and eat. I had started retching. Unable to keep anything down and overcome with the altitude, I felt as if I were underwater dying from lack of air.

I sat in the car for a precious few minutes. John made me an Isagenix shake, watered down and icy. I forced it down, my stomach in turmoil. I felt completely trashed. I couldn't comprehend how I could possibly finish. My energy was gone. Silently Bay and John pulled me out of the van to start moving after a two-minute break. The shake settled my stomach. Now I felt able to walk instead of stagger.

I was cold but it wasn't unbearable. The sun came up as I was halfway up Tang Lang La in deep snow. The view was breathtaking. I suddenly knew at that point that I was going to make it. Until then, I had tried not to think about the prospect of completion but to just keep pushing on. The sun gave me renewed hope and energy. As we approached the summit, I saw some guy doing cartwheels near our support vehicle. I asked Bailey and John if it was our driver. I realized they were questioning my sanity when I saw them exchange looks.

I closed the gap to Samantha Gash and Lisa Tamati and we worked together to get over the mountain as dawn approached. I was hallucinating badly by then, but I knew I wasn't suffering from altitude problems. It was simply extreme fatigue. I can deal with fatigue. It's recoverable.

At the peak of Tang Lang La, a thought entered my head: I might in fact be able to complete the race. I had 18 miles to go—mostly downhill. We'd been on the move for fifty-three hours—two days and two bone-chilling nights. I had survived every type of inclement weather. My entire body inside and out was numb with pain. But if I could simply remain upright and continue moving, I could finish within the allotted time of sixty hours. I wouldn't be the first person to accomplish this reportedly impossible feat, or even the first woman, but I would be the first American woman. I'd never before been first at anything. I kept moving . . . one foot in front of the other . . . even though I was on the verge of collapse with every step.

With the sun shining and the haze in my mind lifted, I was gliding down the mountain. A vehicle coming towards us pulled over and out popped Barry Walton, the videographer. He ran over, embraced

Coming Down from Tang Lang La, mile 119

me, and sobbed. He could not believe that I had caught up with the other runners. He just kept crying and said he had never seen anything like what I had just accomplished. I couldn't stop smiling. I hugged him and told him I'd see him at the finish line.

We ran toward the Morey Plains, the finish line. We had descended out of the snow to the barren mountains with low clouds and thin mist surrounding us. At the finish line Bailey pulled out the American flags we had brought from home. Bailey, John, and I held up our flags and ran to the finish line banner with two hours to go. I was never so proud to wave that flag and be the first American woman to complete La Ultra The High.

At the start of a race of this distance, with challenges so overwhelming, there is no guaranty of finishing. There are too many variables that can take you out in a moment. Finishing this race was so rewarding, and the victory was so sweet, as to be indescribable. For the rest of my life, I will remember the journey I took with Bailey Sheridan, John Vigil, Jigme, and Lamchun. I have never felt so grateful and so happy. Jigme and Lamchun were caring and hard-working. John and Bailey were instrumental—working fifty-eight hours without stopping. I know how hard that was. I owe so much to their devotion. They were also unbelievably funny when I needed a lift.

I simply loved the race, and I love the country of India and its people. The Himalayas are a magic world where the spiritual meets Mother Nature, and it was a blessing to experience the wonders at the ends of the earth.

Finish line—The High, Bailey, me and John

(Barry Walton's documentary *The High* can be found at www.thehighdoc.com)

Finish line, U.S flag

Sharon, me, Rajat, Samatha, Jason, Ray and Lisa

CHAPTER 22

Why?

"The best time to plant a tree was 20 years ago. The second best time is now."
—Chinese Proverb

I FOUND MY life through running. I found pure freedom. I worked through major changes in my life. I found a way to express myself. I overcame fear and found independence. I found courage, strength, and determination that I never thought I possessed. I was following my heart and finding answers to the question: "Who is Molly and what is she capable of?" I always seem to stumble upon the answers to life's difficult questions out in nature, running beneath the open sky.

I want to encourage people to walk and run for health and adventure. Not everyone wants to run, but people can reduce stress through walking. It is calming and peaceful to find a serene trail through the desert or the woods, to take deep breaths, and to walk beneath the trees. Answers are out there waiting for you to discover them.

I know, for myself, I am meant to be running. I'm supposed to be going long distance. That is where my heart tells me to go. I still struggle with my own inadequacies. Running isn't a cure for life's problems. But it helps me with mine.

I found my life through running. I raised my kids and gave everything I had to being the best mother I could. I was awesome. It was everything to me. But then my children grew up and left, just like they are supposed to. All of the energy, nurturing, love, and care that I had given to my kids was ending. My job at work was not enough. What was my purpose? How could I be creative? How could I take all that energy that I had used for my family and improve my life?

It's not about menopause or having a midlife crisis. It is about finding a new purpose in the second act of life. I want to help people get active and expand their minds and be strong physically and mentally.

When I started running, I was bombarded with negativity. A doctor told me I was too old. Friends called me crazy. But they were all wrong. A lot of people are out there floating around. A lot of women are lost and overwhelmed. It especially happens as part of the empty nest syndrome. That isn't menopause. I believe that running, walking, moving, simply getting out in nature, expands a person's mind. Out there, you can find your creativity, your confidence, your strength. You can get your independence back and your sense of self-worth. It is a completely different adventure than raising kids.

I am an average mom who did something out of the ordinary because I summoned all the energy I used as a mother, and turned that to running. To run in impossible circumstances, I needed patience, the endless patience a mother needs when raising her kids. I needed mental strength, the strength a mom needs when she has to deal with a child's illness. A mother seldom uses her talents for herself. She gives and gives and gives. She can forget that she is a powerhouse of wisdom and strength.

When I signed myself up for my very first trail run in Calico, that was the scariest thing I had ever done. I was frightened and intimidated—like a child standing on the high dive for the first time.

But I overcame those fears. In doing so, I gained self-confidence. I achieved a goal which seemed impossible for someone like me. I was proud of myself. I had more courage, more strength, than I had ever realized. Like the child who finally leaps from the high dive, I was beaming with pride and happiness. That experience gave me the confidence to face other intimidating challenges. The entire experience has changed me into a different person . . . a better person.

I could no more stop myself from going on that Himalayan adventure than I could stop breathing. People still ask, "Why did you go? How can you put yourself in such awful circumstances?" I really don't understand those questions. The better question for me is, "How could I NOT go?" All I could think about was adventure . . . adventure . . . adventure.

Epilogue

AS THIS BOOK went to print, I lost my dad. He passed away at ninety years old. My adorable Pop, who was handsome, loveable, an incredible body surfer, who loved all his kids unconditionally.

I received a call from Colleen that he was failing and wasn't expected to make it through the weekend. After hanging up, I immediately called my dad's cell phone, not expecting him to be able to answer. Emphysema had made him weak and slowly taken his health. But his mind was always sharp and fully present. I heard his weak voice on the line.

"Dad! It's me, Molly. How are you doing?"

"Hi, honey," he answered, his words slow and faint, "I'm not doing too well, sweetheart."

"Oh, Dad," my words rushed out, "I love you so much. You are the most wonderful father a girl would ever ask for. I love every moment with you. You have helped me become a better person with all your love and encouragement. Thank you for always being there for me. Thank you for understanding me and loving me unconditionally. Dad, do you want me to come there? I am on my way to a race in Arizona, but I can come to California."

"Honey, you go run. You go run for me. I am surrounded here . . . you run." He sobbed.

"Okay, Pop. I'm taking you with me. You and I are running this weekend." We said our farewells.

I went to the race with a heart that felt like a rock on my chest.

The race was the Javelina Jundred, 100 miles out in the Arizona desert. It was a miserable race for me. I was mentally drained—worried about Dad, hoping he would last a little longer. I prayed to the moon and stars, Mother Earth, Buddha, Jesus, and the angels for Dad. At 3:00 a.m. I stopped and looked up into the vast darkness with a thousand twinkling stars. I suddenly realized that Dad was passing. Tears started spilling down my face as I silently ran and stumbled. I asked for angels to give Dad safe passage to heaven. I ran and cried and tried to conjure up the beautiful life forces of nature to safely send Pop on his way.

After I finished, I walked to my tent. My cell phone was ringing as I pulled back the flap and entered. Colleen was on the phone next to Dad's bed. She told me he had passed away moments before. I sat on my cot and sobbed.

I had run to stir up the energy of the planet, to wake up the angels, to call on God to assist Pop to heaven. Maybe I ran for myself, the only way I could express my sorrow. Pop understood and his last gift to me was helping me deal with his death the only way I knew how. I want to think I helped him on his way. Maybe, by running, I helped us both.

Theodore Wayne Hannegan (Pop)

Additional Author Bio – Al Marquis

Al Marquis is the founding partner of Marquis Aurbach Coffing (www.maclaw.com), a 40 attorney business and real estate law firm in Las Vegas. He has authored hundreds of articles plus two cowboy poetry books: *Frivolous Cowboy Poetry* and *Bucked Bruised & Blackballed*. His latest book, *Cowboy Yoga*, will be available soon. Al lives at Kingston Ranch (www.kingstonranch.com) with his wife Joanie and his best friend, Charlie.

CPSIA information can be obtained at www.ICGtesting.com
Printed in the USA
BVOW10s1428030116

431630BV00003B/6/P